THE CORRECTIONAL COMMUNITY

THE
CORRECTIONAL
COMMUNITY

AN INTRODUCTION AND GUIDE

Edited by

NORMAN FENTON
ERNEST G. REIMER
HARRY A. WILMER

Foreword by

RICHARD A. McGEE

UNIVERSITY OF CALIFORNIA PRESS
BERKELEY AND LOS ANGELES, 1967

University of California Press
Berkeley and Los Angeles, California
Cambridge University Press
London, England
Copyright © 1967, by
The Regents of the University of California
Library of Congress Catalog Card Number: 67-14117

As the administrator of a large state correctional system, I learn about many new developments for the conduct of correctional institutions for youth and adults. All these new methods are interesting. Many offer considerable promise of helping workers in corrections to do their jobs better in assisting offenders to gain lasting benefits from the programs. Studies to help us to better understanding of delinquents and criminals have been aided by the federal government. The contributions of public agencies and private foundations should lead eventually to greater ability on our part to control these restless, unstable, and poorly organized persons and to help them to want to achieve better purposes in life. By turning their energies toward more wholesome and less dangerous living for themselves, they also become thereby less threatening to their neighbors in society. This book is an example of these promising contributions.

Of the many new developments concerning those who enter correctional institutions, none has attracted greater interest than those that aim at using the social forces in the peer group of the offenders for rehabilitation. This book attempts to describe the use of these group methods in the resocialization of inmates. The text gives an introductory account of new methods in institutional treatment which were first tried successfully with patients in mental hospitals and are now being developed for institutionalized offenders. The material has been presented with the restraint that befits an account of a promising but as yet unproved methodology. Those who study it, especially if they have an opportunity to work in an institutional correctional community, will find it interesting, relevant to their work, and of practical value for their professional growth.

The study was sponsored by a training grant from the Office of Juvenile Delinquency and Youth Development, Welfare Administration, U. S. Department of Health, Education, and

Welfare in cooperation with the President's Committee on Juvenile Delinquency and Youth Crime.

The study was prepared under the auspices of the Institute for the Study of Crime and Delinquency in Sacramento, California. As the president of this institute, I hope that the authors and editors of this volume have developed a training resource which will prove to be another step toward preparing the offender to live within the law after his release from the correctional institution.

RICHARD A. MC GEE
Administrator of the
Youth and Adult
Corrections Agency

Sacramento, California
September, 1966

The material in this volume is not presented as a final account of the program called "correctional community," but as a stimulant to the further use and development of a new method. The reader will note occasional repetitions of content, and different emphases, that may help him to gain a many-sided view of the program.

As editors, we had to agree upon a terminology for use in the volume. In earlier and current efforts to evolve a satisfactory nomenclature for this new program, various terms have been used, notably "milieu therapy" and "therapeutic community." These terms have become familiar in describing the transition in the programs of mental hospitals from custodial to therapeutic care.

The term "correctional community" is used here to designate the program as defined in the book and as now used in the correctional institutions for youths and adults in California. In the correctional community, the staff members become better integrated with each other in conducting the treatment program, and communication between staff and inmates is improved. The program attempts to replace the separate inmate and staff value systems by a unified system.

Three terms were selected to designate the basic components of the correctional community: "large group," "small group," and "individual counseling." Their use is now generally accepted by workers in the California institutions. The editors are aware that the therapeutic milieu which evolves from the correctional community can be developed also by methods which may not include large groups. However, the correctional communities, as described in this book, include the large group meetings as a basic component. How often they meet, and for how long, and how they are conducted varies in different institutions.

The fourth term, "post-session," is used here to denote a review or critique by the staff of how the program is developing. Usually, it takes place immediately after the large-group meeting.

This volume was developed during week-end seminars at the Carmel Valley Inn under the auspices of the Training Project in Correctional Methods funded by the Committee on Juvenile Delinquency of the U. S. Department of Health, Education, and Welfare. It was sponsored by the Institute for the Study of Crime and Delinquency of Sacramento, of which Richard A. McGee is president. These sessions, and others elsewhere, led to the planning and fruition of this book for employee training. Authors were selected by the seminar group.

A preliminary draft of the book was submitted to many readers with experience in the correctional community and many constructive suggestions were incorporated.

An Advisory Committee in the Department of Corrections and in the Department of the Youth Authority consisting of (in addition to the authors and editors) Robert H. Donnelly, Tom Scullion, Harold Richard, and Richard C. Kolze made valuable contributions. Consultants invited to the sessions of the committee were Dennie L. Briggs, Frank O'Donnell, and James Robison. Helpful manuscripts on institutional practice were prepared by K. Bazell, Richard B. Heim, R. A. Deal, J. J. Enomoto, R. L. Koehler, Irving Marks, James Park, Tom Scullion, and Weldon H. Smith.

In the Department of Corrections, Director Walter Dunbar took a personal interest and greatly encouraged the editors in their efforts. Deputy Director Lawrence M. Stutsman and the superintendents and wardens of the various departmental facilities assisted in many ways. Alfeo Dal Favero, Assistant Departmental Supervisor of Education, edited part of the text. In the Youth Authority, the interest of Director Heman G. Stark encouraged us. Harry R. Wilson assisted the work of the editors by enlisting the cooperation of staff members in the Central Office of the Youth Authority and the superintendents and other employees in its institutions.

Finally we are grateful for the contributions of Gloria E. Henderson, Evelyn M. Koebig, Lorraine Fontaine, and Natividad Allen of our secretarial staffs for their arduous efforts in the preparation of the volume.

THE EDITORS

CONTENTS

INTRODUCING THE CORRECTIONAL COMMUNITY PROGRAM INTO THE CORRECTIONAL INSTITUTION   *Ernest G. Reimer, M. S. W., Department of Corrections, State of California,* 1

INSTITUTIONAL PREPARATION FOR THE CORRECTIONAL COMMUNITY   *Howard Ohmart, B. S., The Youth and Adult Corrections Agency, State of California,* 13

ADMINISTRATIVE CONSIDERATIONS IN THE CORRECTIONAL COMMUNITY   *Floyd A. Chamlee, A. B., California Institution for Men, Chino, California,* 29

THE NATURE AND FUNCTIONS OF THE COMMUNITY GROUP   *Glynn B. Smith, M. S. W., California Rehabilitation Center, Corona, California,* 52

INMATE GROWTH IN RESPONSIBILITY   *Glynn B. Smith, M. S. W., California Rehabilitation Center, Corona, California,* 72

THE NATURE AND FUNCTIONS OF THE SMALL GROUP   *Norman Fenton, Ph. D., The Training Project in Correctional Methods, Carmel, California,* 85

THE INTERVIEW   *Peter F. Ostwald, M. D.,* 95

THE EVALUATION OF THE CORRECTIONAL COMMUNITY   *John P. Conrad, A. M., Department of Corrections, Sacramento, California,* 107

BIBLIOGRAPHY, 117

Ernest G. Reimer

INTRODUCING THE CORRECTIONAL-COMMUNITY PROGRAM INTO THE CORRECTIONAL INSTITUTION

Inmates in correctional institutions have many unmet needs and many unresolved conflicts. Their behavior may be impulsive; they may respond to feelings and influences without thought for the consequences. They may be hostile and angry toward the staff without knowing or caring to know why they feel as they do. They may have little conception of the necessity for the give and take in normal interpersonal relationships. They commonly have little ability to postpone satisfactions or to plan realistically for the future. However, inmates have many positive aspects in their makeup that permits resocialization through introduction of appropriate new programs, such as the correctional community.

The correctional community is a method of social therapy in which staff and inmates make a conscious effort to utilize all the experiences in all areas of their group eixstence in a therapeutic manner. This program bridges the communication gap between staff and inmates typically found in correctional institutions, and also utilizes inmate peer influence—the self-help concept—to help inmates gain self-awareness and a more responsible outlook. Inmates who live and work together meet with the staff regularly with an expressed goal of improving post-release performance. By employing, under staff direction, open communication, confrontation, as well as other treatment methods, inmate participants can model and adjust their behavior through learning, testing, and fixating newer and more effective modes of perceiving and relating to others.

The correctional community draws from the principles and concepts of the "therapeutic community" initiated by Dr. Maxwell Jones at the Belmont Hospital in London soon after World War II (18). Dr. Jones established a program in which all patients and staff members of one ward in a mental hospital met together daily to discuss, and many times resolve, the living problems of the ward. This approach was based upon the idea that interpersonal difficulties could be resolved through an environment built to focus on problems and their solution.

To understand the effects of the institution on inmates it may be helpful to recall a person's feelings of confinement and lack of self-direction as a patient in a hospital, a soldier in the military service, or even a student in school. We all know how it feels to have our lives subjected to the direction of others. A foremost characteristic of such experiences is the feeling of being treated impersonally. In ordinary life, individuality is usually respected by family and friends. But in large institutions those in charge are usually concerned with the management of the total system rather than the individual.

Inmates and employees feel differently about the institution and its program. Employees spend only part of their daily lives in the institution, but inmates are subject day and night to the impact of the total institutional operation. Inmates see the employees freely come and go, and this freedom drives home to them the restrictions in their own lives.

The staff of an institution influences the inmates' life only in specialized areas, for example, a teacher in a classroom, group supervisors or correctional officers in housing units or recreational areas. If the staff merely do what they are expected to do in the institution in a businesslike, efficient, and impersonal manner, they may co-exist well enough with the inmates. However, there is likely to be little or no communication between staff and inmates due to the lack of empathy and understanding between them. To overcome such psychological barriers, the correctional community has been developed.

The correctional community is a new method of social therapy employed with the expectation that it will prepare inmates better for their return to society. In a correctional community inmates live and work together and have regular community and group meetings with staff. The daily life experiences of the inmates become the subject for group discussion to understand problems in human relations better. Under staff direction communication for the evaluation of oneself and others can be therapeutic. By facing the meaning and the consequences of one's own behavior on fellow community members, it is possible to diminish antisocial tendencies.

In attempting to make the transition from humane but impersonal institutional management to the correctional community, penologists have drawn heavily upon earlier pioneering by workers in mental hospitals. Stanton and Schwartz have given an account of how a mental hospital may make the transition from a humane but largely impersonal institution to a favorable treatment environment. In this book, *The Mental Hospital*, they show how small a part in his life plays the brief period of formal psychiatric treatment the patient receives. Many other influences, beneficial and damaging to the psychiatrist's treatment efforts, improve or disturb a patient's well-being. The authors conclude (31, p. 3): "Our study then is of the hospital as a whole as a highly organized functioning institution in both its formal and informal aspects. It is based upon a reasonable hypothesis that *at least some aspects of the disturbances of the patient are a part of the functioning of the institution*" (italics mine). The troubles among inmates in training schools or prisons and the ineffectiveness of the treatment programs of correctional institutions may similarly stem from the way these institutions are managed.

The correctional institution is usually divided into four separate divisions: custodial care or supervision; accounting or business management; medical-surgical care and hygiene; and classification and treatment. The classification-and-treatment division includes the diagnostic social study of inmates, casework services, academic and vocational education, counseling and psychotherapy, religious guidance, and recreation. The staffs of these separate programs should be aware of each other's goals and methods and be mutually supportive. However, they are often in competition for priority of their functions and for securing primary claim upon the inmates' time. This lack of cooperation is unfortunate, sometimes disastrous. For one thing, the inmates may exploit staff conflicts to gain their advantages through adroit manipulation. Without close and harmonious cooperation of institutional staff, the purpose for which the correctional institution was established will be defeated. When the correctional community is established, one of its purposes is to integrate the various forces in the institution.

HOW THE INSTITUTION AFFECTS THE INMATES

To understand the impact of these competitions it is necessary to try to see the correctional institution from the inmate's point of view. Recently there have been studies by sociologists or psychologists who have lived as if they were patients in mental hospitals. Erving Goffman, in *Asylums* (12), describes "the characteristics of the total institution." He portrays the impersonalizing impact of the total institution on patients or inmates. One example is the "intake process." Goffman portrays the inmate who comes to the institution with a few personal belongings. These things which remind him of himself as a person and of his free-world associates are taken from him "for safekeeping." Besides, he is subjected to the indignity of being stripped to the skin and examined. These and other intake procedures are usually carried out in the presence of other patients. The overtaxed staff can show little consideration to the inmate's feelings. Goffman has aptly called this "the mortification process of intake." The loss of individuality and privacy, that continues throughout the inmate's term, is only the first of many hurts and deprivations of patients in mental hospitals. Inmates arriving at a correctional institution undergo similar experiences. To understand the total process of "institutionalization" of prisoners or "pains of imprisonment" as Sykes (35) refers to them, we must look at these other deprivations.

There is the loss of freedom of activity or self-direction. An inmate is no longer free to eat when, where, or what he wants to eat. He is not free to buy what he wants, where, and when he wants it. He has little or no choice where he will sleep. Usually he is not permitted to perform the simplest acts, such as turning off the light in his room when he wants. Small decisions, like large ones, are usually made for the inmate by others.

A sense of deprivation results from the kind of things given to the inmates for their use. In most state-operated institutions, because of administrative convenience, items are provided as economically as possible and for utilitarian purposes. There is an impersonal sameness in their clothing with little variety in styles or colors. Furnishings in living areas are few. Permission to individualize the decoration of a room or cell may be restricted by institutional regulations. Usually, the only special things an inmate may have are those he may secure for himself at the inmate canteen or what his family may be permitted to bring him.

Services provided are minimal and rarely individualized. The food may be reasonably good, but it may be served unattractively, and the mess hall may be crowded and noisy. The laundry done by inmates is clean but not pressed appropriately.

Another deprivation is the lack of heterosexual relations. Until recently, adult correctional institutions for men had restrictions upon the employment of females so that months could go by without male inmates even seeing or talking to women other than visitors from their family. Even then, in many prisons regulations prohibit a man from kissing his wife when she visits him. In time, this lack of contact with women can have lasting psychological effects.

Another deprivation is the inmate's loss of security; he is subjected to various pressures from his fellow inmates. Prison employees may easily overlook or not understand what it means to live in this population where the average inmate often feels a threat to his safety and even his life from his fellow inmates who may steal, demand with threats canteen purchases, or extort personal possessions. There may be threats of violence from homosexuals. Weaker inmates submit to threats of violence by aggressive fellow inmates. Besides, the unpredictable behavior of those with serious mental illnesses is a source of fear or terror to the inmates. The formal organization of the institution is seldom adequate to protect the individual from his predatory peers. The prison management ordinarily cannot help an inmate to avoid trouble in a correctional institution. He must either pay for protection or take his chances. The group meetings in a correctional community offer the inmate an opportunity to voice his concerns about these deprivations in his prison life. In the community an inmate may find other inmates or staff to help him deal with the frustrations of his daily life.

ADAPTATIONS OF INMATES TO THEIR
INSTITUTIONAL SITUATIONS

Stanton and Schwartz (31) reported a patient-staff ratio much more advantageous for patients in private than in public institutions. In private hospitals, the researchers' study showed, there are almost three employees per patient. In correctional institutions, ratios of one employee to ten or even fifteen inmates are not unusual. Institutional life with an insufficient staff contributes to the inmate's sense of isolation, the feelings of danger and insecurity. Consequently, the adaptations that inmates are forced to make need to be studied.

Many sociologists—Goffman and Sykes, already cited, Schrag (27), Cressey (8), and others—have observed the methods by which inmates adapt to life in correctional institutions.

Inmates who feel lost or hopeless may adapt to the conditions of institutional living in different ways. If they are disturbed by guilt feelings, they tend to suppress them or to explain away any responsibility of their own for being incarcerated. They often project upon others the blame for this condition, thus relieving their sense of guilt. They rationalize their situation and justify their conduct by saying "this is something they did to me and whatever I can get out of this life to justify my own well-being is all right." Thus, the first method of "adaptation" is by projection.

An inmate may try to adapt himself by a second method— by rejecting those who have rejected him. "Society" has removed him from the free world and placed him in confinement. To tolerate this rejection by society, he turns around and rejects the staff of the institution who represent society. This may be the only option available to him to maintain his personal image.

The extreme of adaptation by rejection has been defined by some writers as the "rebel" or, as Schrag (27, p. 8) has called him, the "asocial person." This is the inmate who refuses to conform and is hostile to the staff. He rejects whatever program is offered to him. Frequently he ends up in adjustment centers or segregation units.

Another variation of adaptation by rejection has been referred to as the "antisocial" or the "right guy." His basic identification is with the negative inmate culture or criminal code. He refuses to confide in staff, tends to keep to himself, and conforms only enough to get by. His entire concern is for his own welfare. He wants to complete his term of imprisonment with as little personal discomfort and irritation as possible. When pressed, he will identify with other inmates against staff but prefers not to become involved.

A third method of "adaptation" may be called "situational withdrawal" or denial. An institutionalized inmate may surrender himself to institutional routine and find in this way a comfortable home. He sees himself not in prison being punished, but being taken care of. When an inmate thus surrenders to an institution, the task of preparing him to function in a free society is difficult, if not impossible. He now is dependent upon the institution.

A fourth adaptation has been called by Schrag "prosocial." The inmate adopts the official viewpoint, works at fulfilling the staff expectations, conforms well, identifies with staff, and tries to use the program to advantage.

The fifth type of adaptation has been referred to as the "pseudo-social" or manipulating inmate. He is a "con-man" who makes a show of going along or conforming with the program, but does so only superficially. Beneath the surface, he remains a self-centered individual uninterested in the institutional programs for self-improvement.

The inmates' adaptations are influenced more by their peers than by the staff and the program of the institution. For every hour that an inmate is subjected to the influences of staff members, the influences of other inmates affect him for many hours. For every hour inmates spend in treatment, they spend countless hours with one another in "bull sessions" usually cast in negative values.

It may be stated that the inmates impose their value systems and standards of behavior on correctional institutions. These are formidable barriers to the rehabilitative programs. The inmate value system in an institution is called the "inmate culture" or the "inmate code." This self-imposed system is an effective means of controlling the inmates' behavior and thinking in the institution. It is also an attempt to escape from control of the staff.

THE INFORMAL ORGANIZATION OF AN INSTITUTION

The subcultures of the staff and the inmates exist side by side in the institution. The informal inmate organization is a serious handicap to the staff's efforts toward resocialization of the inmates. Several authors have shown how the inmate subculture is a means of reconciling the inmates to their painful situation as prisoners in what Sykes has called "the society of captives."

Conflict between inmates and staff arise because of staff efforts directed toward the security of the institution and the attempt at constructive rehabilitation programs. Conflicts occur and are readily observed in crowded mess halls and large congregate housing units.

Another feature that makes for the development of this informal inmate organization is the role assumed by the correctional employee. He spends most of his working day with the inmates. As shown by Sykes (35, p. 6), the correctional worker is isolated from other staff members and from the formal administration of the institution and therefore often lacks identification with the administration of the institution. He may over-sympathize with the inmates, and begin to think like them. Since they are more closely associated with the inmates than with the administration of the institution, it is not unusual to observe that correctional employees, for their own welfare and protection, rely upon the inmates to carry out the routine operations of the institution. This is especially true when staffing is inadequate; although economical on budgets, understaffing is extravagantly expensive in that it fosters antitherapeutic cultures.

The correctional worker, like all men, desires to be liked, and therefore may make compromises on strict obedience to the institutional rules. He may overlook minor infractions by inmates to avoid resentment, rejection, or hostility and thereby increase the difficulties and dangers of his work. In the adult correctional institution described by Sykes, the informal organization of the prison was a major factor in the life of the custody-oriented institution. The management of the institution had developed its plans or programs primarily for administrative needs with only a token effort in the way of a treatment program for the inmates. In the daily operations of this maximum-custody institution, efforts toward resocialization were secondary. The primary effort was for the staff and the inmates to compromise on a way of life.

This compromise in institutional operation was supported by both the inmate and the employees. The institution was involved in a "cold war" situation. The two sides agreed informally upon certain rules of the game to assure reasonably safe co-existence. On the surface, the goals of the staff and the inmates appear to be reconciled; actually they continue to be different. When any attempt is made by the staff members to force their point of view on the inmates, the result has usually been open conflict. Until the open-forum features of the correctional community were developed, there had been no systematic, effective means of communication between the two groups, except for the very limited means of inmate advisory bodies.

The informal organization of correctional institutions applies to institutions for youths. The human forces and interpersonal relationships in a well-staffed private training school for disturbed youths between ages 12 and 17 have been described in Howard Polsky's (23), *Cottage Six*. His book admirably portrays the social structure of the cottage in an institution in which the more difficult boys were housed. He also notes the relationships between the boys in Cottage Six and those elsewhere in the institution.

The cottage life and the training or treatment activities of the institution were administratively separate. Cottage Six was a separate and isolated operation during two-thirds of the week. As a consequence, Cottage Six, being largely controlled by a hierarchy of power distributed among the youthful inmates, developed its own culture and administration in the day-by-day operations of the cottage. Polsky describes this hierarchy by the term "pecking order." The social structure and the distribution of authority were based on the strength and domination of inmate subgroups or cliques. The top boys in this hierarchy were the leaders or "the toughs." They were the best fighters. From among their peers in the cottage they recruited a group of lieutenants who supported their administration, resorting, when necessary, to brutality. This power group was followed in the pecking order by a second group, the "con-artists" or the manipulators. The third group, the "quiet boys," was composed of passive individuals, and the fourth group of the "weaklings," or the "bush boys." At the bottom of the pecking order were the "scapegoats" and the "punks."

The pecking order was rigid in composition and operation. Boys in the different levels were kept in their places by the leaders. This social order changed only when one boy was released from Cottage Six, which resulted in a general movement upward among the others to fill his spot in the hierarchy.

The informal organization of the cottage was often enlarged by the relationships of the male-female employee team of "cottage parents or supervisors" to the inmates. The middle-class "cottage parents" were individuals who had frequently been unsuccessful in previous vocational pursuits. Polsky describes how "cottage parents" accommodated themselves to the informal social structure of the cottage. A way of cottage life developed with the employees maintaining certain supervisory roles. The boys in the cottage cooperated with the "cottage parents" as long as these accepted the informal structure as the actual government of the cottage. Life for the employees in the cottage was kept reasonably peaceful and orderly by the inmate leaders as long as the cottage parents accepted the leaders' roles.

One factor that aided this working arrangement between the cottage parents and the inmates was the feeling of isolation of the former because of their functional separation from the rest of the institutional staff. The employees in the cottages were concerned primarily with maintaining order. Because they did not feel involved in the main stream of the treatment and training purposes of the institution, they felt compelled to compromise with what might be called good "moral" training.

Some inmates were conscious of being the victims of the rigid informal organization in the cottage. They would have preferred a different social structure, offering more constructive benefits. But because the cottage parents were not inclined to change the social structure, the boys likewise had to compromise by adhering to the existing structure with its tyrannies of the pecking order.

THE DILEMMA OF THE CORRECTIONAL INSTITUTION

The disturbed emotional characteristics of the population and the organizational shortcomings of the correctional institution combined to militate against the rehabilitation, training, and treatment programs for the inmates. The summary chapters of the books by Sykes and Polsky describe this dilemma.

Polsky (23, chap. 10) has summarized the influence of social interaction patterns on the inmates as follows:

Our analysis this far has amply demonstrated that whatever impact Hollymead (the total institution) has upon individual boys, as a whole the boys are mightily influenced by the patterns of social interaction, into which they enter day after day. These social patterns are in turn a part of a complex social system of roles, norms, values, and methods of control. Any effort to rehabilitate youngsters will be sharply conditioned by these social systems of sub-groups, cliques, cottage units and institutions. The extent to which they can change, the extent to which we really want to change them, these are the important issues in addition to the individual psychopathology.

Sykes (35, chap. 7) summarizes the inmate subculture and its significance for the operation of the institution in these words:

The crux of imprisonment is the social interactions prisoners indulge in day after day, month after month. This results in a social system and the extent to which this social system functions to help or harm the inmate and the extent to which we can modify or control the social system and the extent to which we are willing to change it, these are issues which confront us and not the recalcitrance of the individual inmate.

Polsky (23, chap. 11) has summarized what needs to be done this way:

In setting the goals of residential treatment as a reintegration of the resident into the community, we must not forget that both sides of the transaction are important, individual resident and community Whatever the boys' psychopathology, they must relate to social patterns made appropriate for them by the peer culture. Individual boys who adjust to the cottage are in effect conforming to a deviant society in which destructive values and social patterns have been raised to a virtue by which status can be attained. The fundamental task of a residential treatment center is not only to rehabilitate individual youngsters, but to create a therapeutic youth culture, the latter mediates institutional values and exerts a profound influence upon each boy.

INSTITUTIONAL PREPARATION FOR THE CORRECTIONAL COMMUNITY

In California, it was the correctional institutions for adults which have been the scene of most of the experimental efforts to use the correctional community as a method of institutional treatment. However, reports of experiences in two institutions of the California Youth Authority—the Paso Robles School for Boys and the Preston School of Industry (11)—confirm that the correctional community may be readily adapted for use in juvenile and youth institutions as well.

CATEGORIES OF PROGRAM DEVELOPMENT IN CORRECTIONAL INSTITUTIONS

There is a marked difference between an institution conducted as a correctional community and institutions using other concepts. Vinter and Janowitz (36), in their investigations of public and private juvenile correctional schools, prepared a rough rating schedule. Their schemes or method apply equally well to reformatories and prisons. They rank the institutions according to programs as follows:

Confinement or Containment-Oriented Institutions. — The chief concern of these institutions is with discipline, control, and suppression of delinquent activity within their confines. There is little communication and a maximum of separation or "social distance" between inmates and staff.

Training-Oriented Institutions. — These institutions specialize in academic and vocational training. Those in charge believe that discipline combined with trade training and hard work will lead to the formation of good behavior. Somewhat greater inmate-staff communication than in the first program is brought about by the instruction. However, there is still considerable social distance between inmates and staff.

Transitional Institutions. — These institutions are moving toward an emphasis upon treatment. Vinter and Janowitz noted that institutions in transition struggle with program direction and reveal a conflict between the older methods of training through discipline and "work for work's sake" and the newer methods of treatment designed to affect constructively the attitudes of the children and youth under their care.

Treatment-Oriented Institutions. — In these institutions traditional individualized psychotherapy is stressed. Other facets of the program play subordinate roles. Vinter and Janowitz did not regard this type of institution as the solution for resocializing delinquents, because of its excessive concern with two people—therapists and individual subjects. Although a greater degree of permissiveness is evident, the relationships among inmates, among staff members, and between inmates and staff are not significantly better than in the third type.

Milieu-Treatment Institution. — Milieu treatment may be characterized as a "total institutional treatment climate." Vinter and Janowitz regarded these places as the most advanced. In this category fall the institutions in which the correctional community has been introduced. Under capable leadership, each member of the staff is accorded a treatment role, and the relationships among inmates, between inmates and staff, and among staff members, is potentially the most satisfactory.

PREPARATION FOR THE THERAPEUTIC COMMUNITY

We concur in the belief that the treatment program integrated into a community-oriented institution represents the most advanced form of institutional operation. Such operations are so recent that a sufficient statistical evaluation does not yet exist.

Administrators of institutions for younger inmates, who are contemplating the introduction of correctional communities, ask questions, such as:

Will the model developed largely in the California reformatories and prisons serve our needs?

Would the psychological differences between children or younger adolescents and and adults influence a juvenile institution to modify this model?

Is there a minimal age of institutional inmates below which they are not capable of adapting to the correctional community?

In a youth institution, administrators and advisers should realize that modifications are necessary in accordance with the needs of the inmates and the experience of the staff in terms of their skills and training in the correctional-community concept. Although additional employees may eventually be needed, we believe that the initial development of a correctional-community program should take place in the present physical arrangements of the institution and with its present staff. In introducing this program into any institution, whether for older youths or adults or for juveniles, some special local adjustments may have to be made, however. Some general suggestions for this are found in chapter iii, and they apply to all types of correctional institutions.

PRACTICAL CONSIDERATIONS

An administrator must first identify the objectives of his own institution that coincide with the program's purposes. The objectives of most correctional systems are to protect society by substituting training and treatment toward rehabilitation for retributive punishment of young persons. This objective is regarded not only as helpful to them in staying out of trouble, but also in finding satisfaction in individual and group achievements.

We might say that the objective is to make nondelinquents of delinquents; that is, to provide opportunities for physical, intellectual, and emotional growth toward maturity. This greater maturity will be realized when the inmate has the ability to live harmoniously with his fellows, to develop self-control, to be law-abiding, to participate productively in the life of the institution rather than remain a hostile self-centered deviant. Greater maturity will enable the individual to forego immediate satisfaction of needs in the interest of greater, long-term advantages. Immature persons, such as children, are short-sighted. Maturity includes the ability to curb strong, anti-social impulses and to find satisfaction in wholesome achievements.

In introducing the correctional community, the staff must resist the temptation of duplicating existing patterns. Each institution must tailor its program to its own resources. The differences between small and large institutions are such that correctional communities should also be presumed to differ.

Further, the staff must recognize the importance of training. Instruction in the goals and general activities of the correctional community should begin *before* the program is started. Training must be continuous. For example, one of the significant goals of the Training Project in Correctional Methods (11), of which this book is an outcome, has been to instruct staff in the theory and practice of the correctional community. While they studied the theory, they were at the same time participating in correctional communities in their own institutions. After the program was started, it seemed advantageous to present the theoretical concepts and relate them to on-the-job practice in the training of staff.

Finally, the initial correctional community project should be restricted to one or two of the better staffed housing units. The pilot program, given a favorable chance, may be extended. Staff members who are not going to participate in the initial programs should be kept well informed of the program while they continue to maintain their customary activities. Those conducting programs in education, maintenance, religion, recreation, and other institutional operations will have to become integrated with, and be supportive of, the correctional community if the program is to be successful. In the meantime, the concern of the administrative staff will be to see that those engaged in other programs of training and treatment do not become competitive with the development of the community. Through planned in-service training, their activities should become integrated into the new over-all objectives of the institution. In the correctional community, all members of the staff should try to understand and eventually to commit themselves to these new concepts, and participate in the program.

One argument in favor of the correctional community is its potential value for employees as well as for inmates. It offers to members of the staff the opportunity to "see themselves as others see them." While this may be painful or uncomfortable, it will contribute to an improved institutional environment. The staff members may develop an awareness of their own areas of potential growth. They will have the opportunity to become more sensitive to the behavior of colleagues, as well as inmates, and understand better why and in what way these may differ from their own.

The harmony of the institution and the consequent greater well-being of the staff has been, we believe, an important outcome of the correctional community, primarily because channels of frank, spontaneous, meaningful communication are opened between staff and inmates. Employees learn about the effects of their ways upon their charges. Inmates learn what their behavior means to the staff. We may conclude then that for all concerned, staff and inmates alike, mutual help toward personal growth through better communication is an important value of the correctional-community program. The values derived from improved inmate and staff communication are worth stressing. According to Vinter and Janowitz, greater separation or social distance between inmates and staff are characteristic of the less advanced institutions.

The three principal elements of the correctional-community program, the large group, the small group, and individual counseling will be discussed in separate chapters but a sketch of each may be of help at this point. Of the three, the large group or, as it is sometimes called, the "community group," is the principal tool of the correctional community. Some contend that the other two are of secondary importance. They believe that the small group, and particularly individual counseling, become competitive with the large group and detract from its effectiveness. We need greater experience and careful experimentation before we can resolve the questions of priority of the three forms.

The large-group meeting is attended by inmates of a dormitory or of a section of a housing unit. Such groups have been used successfully in juvenile, youth, and adult institutions. It is essential that all members of the staff participate regularly in these meetings, and in the "post-sessions" or staff discussions.

The small group is attended by a staff leader and ten to fifteen inmates. It is more readily understood because of the growing popularity of two procedures. The first is group therapy as practiced by clinical specialists in psychiatry, psychology, or social work with about ten or fifteen inmates. The second is group-counseling which, in correctional systems in California and elsewhere, is conducted with groups of the same size by correctional workers of all job classifications.

Individual counseling or casework needs no definition.

As a result of better communication, relationships among the participants improve. Inmates in the large and small groups can be observed to change in their attitudes toward each other because of the common commitment to and identification with the group or the community. Greater mutual acceptance usually develops among all participants in the correctional community. This mutual commitment to a common, constructive objective is the basis for breaking the undesirable patterns of relationships as described in the preceding chapter. Commitment to a common goal may be illustrated by the thoughtful group resolution of some problems in the operation of the institution. Or, the group may analyze a member's behavior as it affects others. The group may discuss other problems likely to be encountered by those to be released. If the correctional-community communications are sincere and candid, individuals develop a tolerance of others despite differences.

THE VALUES OF "ACTIVITY GROUPS"

In addition to the mentioned group activities used in the correctional community, there are other group activities organized around special areas of interest, such as hobbies, dramatics, athletics, or music. Also, on specific occasions a group of youths with a staff leader are engaged in an activity purposefully directed toward a mutually acknowledged goal, such as, for example, fighting a forest fire. These group experiences in a forestry camp can result in better communication, greater mutual interest, respect and good will, and some of the other values achieved in the correctional community groups. Construction projects, planned by inmates and staff working together, are further examples.

"Activity groups" do not rely as extensively on verbal interaction. Since many inmates are verbally not skilled, activity groups offer them ways of establishing relationships not dependent on verbal skill. These groups also permit the staff to reach the nonverbal individual by an experience comparable to the initial socialization of the preverbal child in the family. The relationships with authority figures in a goal-oriented group activity facilitates nonverbal and verbal communication between the inmates and staff. To a degree, these activity groups may counteract the delinquent influences. We believe that more use should be made of activity groups to supplement and complement the treatment program in institutions conducted according to the principles of the correctional community.

Activity groups are not intended to explore the inmate's personal problems but to offer him the opportunity to examine his attitudes and feelings in the group. They offer practical experiences in cooperative living and tasks which require structured activities and relationships; they contribute to an inmate's self-control, pleasure, and group achievement which can be continued in life after confinement.

However, most inmates need individual or group treatment to face their feelings and life experiences. They need to explore with others the consequences of past and present behavior and the relationship of the two. The group processes of the correctional community which facilitate this self-awareness are necessary for their resocialization. Therefore, the values of activity groups are magnified when they are used in conjunction with the correctional-community program.

THE CORRECTIONAL COMMUNITY AND
THE HOUSING-CENTERED PROGRAM

For the past several years, many California correctional facilities have taken the first step toward creation of the correctional-community program. They have been emphasizing the staff-team concept with the organization of functioning groups of employees who work closely with individual inmates. These include the housing supervisors, teachers, counselors, and tradesmen.

The forerunners of the housing-unit type of organization which integrates all housing-unit staff, are such administrative devices as the Housing Classification or Program Evaluation committees. These devices allow staff members and others to meet periodically to assess the programs of individual inmates. A staff team functions as a decision-making group when it plans an inmate's program or submits recommendations concerning his release.

Staff organization moves toward the community-living concept when teachers are assigned to teach exclusively the boys in one cottage. These living units develop a character and identity, thus becoming a focus of the living-program organization. Other facets of the training and treatment program should later be organized to correlate with programs already established.

The group supervisor plays a key role in the housing-centered program of the correctional community. He has more contact than others and, hence, potentially the greatest impact on the individual and the group. Studies, which have probed the inmate's perception of institutional operations, have shown consistent findings—it is "the man"—the inmate's term for group supervisor, who looms as most important to them as they look at their lives in the institution. This information supports the move to strengthen the role of the group supervisor, to upgrade his skills and practices, and to recognize his core function.

In the living unit a certain value system, a "culture," originates, and inmate social relationship and a hierarchy of status are established. In the living unit originates the cruel "pecking order" which gives over much of the autocratic control of the cottage to the inmates themselves because the staff desires peace and orderliness. The inmate culture may become a powerful force opposing the administration and purpose of the institution and all concerned with it. As illustrated by the living group described by Howard Polsky in *Cottage Six* (23), this delinquent culture may diminish or negate the resocialization efforts of the institutional educational or social psychiatric programs.

In the youth and adult institutions of California, the living units have been selected as the locales of the psychologic social battleground between the delinquency-dominated inmate society and the correctional community. But, obviously, the battle areas cannot be limited entirely to the housing unit. To achieve maximum impact, the staff team must operate everywhere in the institution in a mutually supportive environment with a common understanding of the needs of the individual inmate whenever they encounter him. The staff-team plans bases its program on the answers to these questions: Is the inmate an immature, insecure, dependent individual who needs continual support, encouragement, patience, and tolerance? Or, is he aggressive in behavior and words, a "con-man" who needs to be controlled and reminded that others are aware of his manipulative methods? Or, is he a fairly mature youth anxious about his delinquent patterns, and needing an opportunity to talk about them and, if possible, to understand why he has broken the law? Everyone on the staff in close association with inmates must think and act, as much as possible, in accordance with an individualized program for each of them upon which they have all agreed. The correctional community minimizes the number of staff members with whom an inmate has a significant relationship. This relationship is intensified because the few members of the staff team who deal with the inmate personally are the same persons with whom he is in contact outside the housing unit. The correctional community introduces the values of a small institution by using the housing unit as the focus of the treatment program.

TRANSITION TO THE STAFF TEAM

After an inmate is received at a California correctional institution, a group of staff members study the personal reports about him and interview him. This classification group consists of staff members who will be responsible for planning his institutional programs. The classification personnel usually include the housing supervisor, the classification counselor, representatives of academic and vocational education, the athletic coach, the chaplain, and occasionally others. If the inmate presents psychological problems, the social worker or psychologist in charge of his case participates in the classification discussion.

Before the classification session, the staff will have received the individual's clinical report from the Reception-Guidance Center. They will have various impressions of the inmate as a result of their initial observations of him. The group discussion in the classification conference is aimed at evolving an agreement about the preferred program for the inmate.

The results of this program are later reviewed. All staff members contribute to a cumulative record of the youth's performance. A log or hand-written notebook for each inmate keeps this record. Access to this continuous record minimizes the number of staff meetings necessary for reviewing the youth's progress. In the intervals between classification sessions, this record is available to keep staff members aware of his progress and problems. At quarterly intervals, as a rule, the classification group meets again and makes a general assessment of the progress shown and the current strengths and deficiencies of the inmate, and discuss program changes. To be effective, the inmate should participate in the discussion when the staff is considering his program. These records are of value in determining decisions regarding future programming for the inmate.

The classification meetings may be seen as the instrument through which the impact of the program can be made consistent and mutually supportive among the personnel and programs of the institution. If the classification group agrees in their recommendations for individual and group treatment of the inmate, if he is permitted to participate in part of their deliberations to develop plans for his own program, then he may perceive and understand them, thus contributing to the effectiveness of his treatment program. The attitudes of the staff as they deal individually and collectively with the inmate, the degree to which he is genuinely involved in the proceedings and the decision-making, will all contribute to or detract from the therapeutic quality of the total institutional climate as the inmate perceives it. And it is the nature of his perception of it that is the reality for the individual.

The development and smooth functioning of the classification group is an important preliminary step in the evolution of an institutional correctional community. At the youth institutions in Preston and Paso Robles, the staff teams consist of employees who are immediately concerned with the inmate's life and program. The staff team meets in the cottage whereas the classification committee meets somewhere else, usually in the Administration Building. The senior group supervisor conducts staff-team sessions, attended by teachers, correctional counselors, and others. The boy is brought in and permitted to discuss his program with the staff team. If the morale of the group is good, it will strengthen and support the inmate after the program begins and anxieties and difficulties appear. The agreement of the staff regarding the individual inmate's program helps in its consistent integrated development. For example, different elements in the program, such as education, dormitory supervision, or recreation become mutually supportive under this arrangement.

The correctional-community value goes beyond the classifi-

24   INSTITUTIONAL PREPARATION

cation group and develops a staff team. This is a pattern of
institutional organization growing up around the housing unit
and including the line personnel. It serves to integrate the different phases of the training and treatment program. It enables
the juvenile or adult correctional institution to advance from a
collection of separate programs to an integrated one in which
all levels of personnel have roles. It makes possible a high
form of what Vinter and Janowitz call the "milieu level" of
institutional operation.

PARALLELS, DIFFERENCES IN YOUTH
AND ADULT INSTITUTIONS

Differences between children, youths, and adults will influence
the ways in which institutions are conducted for inmates of
different ages, and also how the correctional community develops. Emotions are closer to the surface in a child or adolescent
than in an adult. Between puberty and adulthood, the adolescent is in a period of biological and social stress with consequent instability. He faces a crucial dilemma. On the one hand,
he longs for dependency, to have someone genuinely concerned about him and available for help in times of need; he
seeks the comforts of a dependent sheltering relationship with
an accepting adult. On the other hand, he strives for independence, for success and achievement by himself and for self-
sufficiency.

Most delinquents have been unsuccessful in this search for
the "good parent," who would provide support and, at the
same time, allow some independence. Instead, they have found
an answer to their dependency needs in the acceptance and
the kind of security offered by relationships with delinquent
peers. The delinquent gang fulfills a need for belonging. This
group may flaunt their emancipation from childhood dependency by defying social customs in dressing differently or by
defying adult rule in antisocial behavior.

Man at all ages is a social being largely influenced in his
beliefs and actions by his fellow men. Loyalty and responsive-
ness to peers is particularly characteristic of adolescents. Strict

compliance with the customs and rituals of the peer group has been considered one of the predominant characteristics of the adolescent culture. It may be evident in fads, peculiar behavior, and overt or covert defiance. The conflict about conformity explains in part why the antisocial standards of his delinquent peers are so important in the life of the institutionalized inmate. Not able to conform to one social system which rejects him or he rejects, he conforms to one he accepts and which willingly accepts him.

Being neither a child nor an adult when committed, the adolescent has been rejected by the legitimate social structure and "sent away" to a correctional institution. He now may have no choice in being forced into dependence upon his delinquent peers. Thus, he may develop an increasing antipathy for adults and for the programs they prescribe for him. The strength of these feelings was revealed by the reaction of a delinquent girl encountered by a visitor in a new and beautifully furnished institutional living room. When the visitor commented pleasantly, "What a lovely room this is," she answered with disdain, "You can have it." Strong resentment toward their captors and what they try to do is a handicap to treatment. Peer group loyalty enhances this reaction.

Paradoxically, this group loyalty may be used to help the youthful delinquent to be more responsive as therapeutic group processes begin to work. His wholesome responses to group pressures under favorable circumstances may be as great as they are under unfavorable circumstances. His residual strong but denied dependency needs, his unexpressed hunger for security and acceptance explain this paradox. These feelings may be met in a therapeutic community group of his peers, especially if he becomes convinced of the sincerity of the leaders conducting the group. If his peers are predominantly in accord with the objectives of a program like the correctional community, he too is probably in accord.

Emotional outbursts may occur in the delinquent adolescent deprived of security in his earlier life. To the extent then that the correctional community's operation is dependent on its members acting maturely, the youthful community might be expected to operate under greater handicaps than the adult community. But since the group processes are designed to permit outspoken irrational feeling as well as rational reactions, the volatile emotions of institutionalized inmates may actually be a helpful factor.

STAFF RESISTANCE TO THE CORRECTIONAL COMMUNITY

The ratio of staff to inmates is usually greater in juvenile institutions than in those for adults. There are more teachers, clinicians, counselors, and social workers. Many of these professionals are attempting to fulfill roles they learned in agencies other than correctional institutions. Those dedicated to individual psychotherapy may object to the emphasis on group methods in the correctional community. These clinicians may be resistant and feel threatened when a question is raised whether treatment is solely their province. They may be unwilling to relinquish their pre-eminent professional stature and accept the participation of the entire staff as equal colleagues in the treatment program. To be candid, the protection of vested interests, the evidences of professional jealousy and status, and other sources of resistance may show themselves when the correctional community is first considered and during the initial period of its introduction. Sometimes nonprofessional staff members wish to move too fast and beyond their competence and are unwilling to confide their own feelings of inadequacy, thus deprecating the professional.

Other professionally trained staff members, notably teachers, also present objections to taking part in the large group or other features of the correctional community. Some teachers tend to reject this kind of treatment role, insisting that they are instructors, not counselors. Some academic and vocational teachers may be seriously threatened by the group-treatment strategies of the correctional community which make it necessary for them to work as colleagues with less educated members of the cottage staff. Hence, the possibility of intelligent and articulate resistance to the community-treatment methods may be enhanced by the objections raised by the more generous staffing of the juvenile institution with clinicians and other academically trained employees. In truth, whenever one changes established traditions, and when experienced people are asked to perform new roles and tasks in which they doubt their own competency, they resist change with its uncertainties and unfamiliar demands.

Some work foremen resist when asked to attend a group meeting, because their own crews, like the students who are kept from their lessons, must be off the job for an hour or more during the short work day. The horizons of busy work foremen extend only to the completion of their assignments to finish a construction job, to meet plumbing crises, or clean the administration building. Lastly, some dormitory supervisors resent having their customary custodial roles changed by required attendance at group meetings. Moreover, they may not relish the requirement to participate in such meetings and are threatened by the leadership roles expected of them. Behind fears of each of these types of people and their functioning role is the concern of being exposed, being criticized openly, and of relinquishing the protective elements of established hierarchical systems.

It is, therefore, of paramount importance that all members of the staff be informed as early as possible during the planning stages of the reasons for any necessary changes in program or administration. They should also be consulted about the details of the future operation if the necessary teamwork is to be achieved.

Inmates resist the correctional community especially when it is called a "treatment" method. Moreover, they are perplexed by the new role of the dormitory supervisors. Not only does the staff face difficulties in the modifications in their roles, but inmates of all ages also have fixed patterns of behavior and prejudices and need to be fully informed beforehand about the proposed changes necessitated by the correctional community.

In balancing this account, we may note many favorable factors in advancing the introduction of the correctional community. For example, many professionals have been eager to experiment with this promising treatment program; and have provided essential leadership for the correctional-community programs in youth and adult institutions. Finally, the correctional or supervisory workers in the living units and elsewhere have welcomed the opportunity to be recognized as constructive forces in the treatment of inmates with whom they have to deal for long hours every working day. When properly prepared for the program, housing supervisors have usually shown enthusiastic interest in the correctional community.

FLOYD A. CHAMLEE

ADMINISTRATIVE CONSIDERATIONS IN THE
CORRECTIONAL COMMUNITY

FIRST STEPS

The administrative staff of an institution should make a number
of preparations before attempting to establish the correctional
community. The staff should read the best material available
and engage in discussions of the theory and practices of the
correctional community. Simultaneously, staff members should
visit and spend some time in a well-functioning correctional
community. This will give them an opportunity to talk to other
administrators, to those in immediate charge of the unit, and
to the inmates. These steps should help the staff to understand
the correctional-community concept, and to determine whether
they wish to proceed with the project.

When the institutional staff decide to introduce the correctional community, their next steps would be to explain the
program to the inmate population; to define the size and location of the initial demonstration unit or units; and to determine
the types of inmates to participate and the methods by which
they will be selected. The plans should consider also the avail-
ability of professional consultants and decide whether research
should be part of the program. While these are being defined
it will be necessary to indicate how the project will be staffed
and what financial and other resources will be made available.
Next would be the preparation of statements for the information of the staff regarding the administration of the project; and
the preparation of a practical program of in-service training.

ADJUSTMENTS IN ADMINISTRATIVE ATTITUDES

It is important that top and middle management support the program. Ideally, the supervisor who is head of the correctional community should report directly to the head of the institution. However, the supervisor must solicit the cooperation of his colleagues inside and outside the correctional community.

In California the top administrative leadership of the Department of Corrections favored the introduction of the correctional community. Two unusual occurrences took place in the Pine Hall Dormitory project at the California Institution for Men. They illustrated the demands of this new program upon the patience of these leaders in corrections whose responsibilities to the public would influence them to expect their subordinates to abide by tradition. One instance occurred during a period of inmate-staff conflict in the Pine Hall community when the deputy director of Corrections visited. Several inmates, to demonstrate their hostile attitudes toward the staff, chose not to make their beds, knowing that this was an infraction of departmental rules. The second incident occurred the same week, when the superintendent of the institution visited the disorderly dormitory and also attended the community-group meeting. The inmates during this session confronted the supervisor with their opinions of his inadequacies. One of them said he felt the supervisor was "sicker than some of the inmates."

The deputy director and the superintendent were both sufficiently alert to withhold judgment with regard to the program. Although uncomfortable in the situation, they were willing to accept the supervisor's comment that the incidents were not beyond his control and that in a positive sense he believed that the results would lead to an increase in maturity among the individuals involved; that the incidents were of potential value in enabling the inmates to understand their hostilities. By helping them work through their feelings, by letting them study why they felt and behaved as they did, order did return and the community was strengthened in dealing constructively with other delinquent wishes and behavior in the future.

Tolerance, understanding, and forbearance of behavior contrary to the standards of conventional correctional management is also required of the staff of the community program. They must be prepared for frustrations and hostilities and if they cannot live with the frustrations occasioned by this behavior and feel compelled to resort to traditional methods of coping with it, they might stimulate additional hostility.

A BROADER ORGANIZATIONAL STRUCTURE

In addition to the necessity for some assurance of top administrative support, there is also need for a definite, organizational structure within the correctional community. There should be a direct line of responsibility to the supervisor in charge of the correctional community from the staff engaged in the unit's operations. The supervisor should have primary responsibility for the selection and removal of staff.

The purpose of this organizational structure is to create a consistent treatment philosophy. The supervisor of the unit should be able to develop a total network of staff communication, and integrate the management of the correctional community. The staff members who supervise the inmates should be in communication with one another, and should have conferences to implement treatment plans. They should bring to the group observations of the behavior of the inmates. Anything of significance revealed to them by the inmates should be communicated to others on the staff. Supervisors should be willing to listen to their staff and their candid opinions and be able to correct deficiencies.

Good communications between the supervisor and the head of the institution are essential so that they may agree on what innovations are acceptable. The head of the institution should be kept aware of developments in the correctional community through regular conferences with the supervisor and periodic attendance at the community meetings. He may assign a representative to the program but he should not delegate his basic responsibility.

THE CONTROL OF DEVIATIONS

As we have stressed earlier, the institutional administration in which a correctional community is established should appreciate the unusual nature of some innovations that are a part of the program. The supervisor and his staff in the correctional community have a continual concern to find ways to provide inmates with opportunities for growth through group interaction, enabling them within limits to assume responsibility for their own conduct. What can be done to accomplish these purposes will be developed somewhat differently in each correctional community.

The following policy was established in one institution to try to work this out amicably: "Any proposed deviations from existing written institutional or departmental policies or procedures must first be submitted in writing." In meeting the requirements of this directive, the supervisor of the correctional community had to give full particulars, including his justifications for any variations from ordinary regulations. In his statement, he was also expected to outline the custodial and other safeguards he proposed to use. Through this means and other routine reporting, the administration could be kept informed about the unit. Supplementary conferences and explanations may be necessary to clarify fully what is proposed, but administrative sanction can usually remain fairly constant and strong. However, all should recognize that such a plan can only be maintained to a certain point. There should be leeway for the staff of the community to vary from the agreed-upon administrative procedures when an emergency requires it. The administration should be informed as soon as possible about the emergency and the nature of the unexpected deviation from the earlier agreement.

THE LOCATION OF THE CORRECTIONAL COMMUNITY

In a state correctional system, different institutions are provided for the various kinds of inmates. A forestry camp or a minimum-custody institution is more adapted for the introduction of the correctional community than housing units in large, maximum custody, walled institutions. The isolated locale of a camp would pose fewer problems for the correctional community. In the large institution, problems of administration would not be easily resolved. Instead of the unit being autonomous in its operation, an institutional location would require the usual intervening hierarchy of staff between the superintendent and the supervisor of the unit. Even if the supervisor of the unit were to report directly to the head of the institution, there would still be more restrictions in the institution than in the isolated camp. In the latter, the program could be carried out with less interference. Unless some unusual condition arose affecting the public welfare, the supervisor of the community unit in the camp would have greater leeway in his operations.

In contrast, the supervisor heading a unit in a dormitory in a large institution, even if he reported directly to the head of the institution, would be under the constant observation of others on the supervisory staff. In some places where the community program has been tried, many middle-management officials have expressed openly skepticism about the program. Their backgrounds of training and experience make it understandably difficult for them to accept new programs.

Wherever located, the unit selected for the correctional community should be somewhat apart from the rest of the institution. A separate barracks or a wing of a housing unit are good locations. The unit must have a room large enough for the entire group to meet and must provide privacy. In the large institutions, issues will arise in the correctional community which may affect other units of the institution. To meet these issues, the staff will need to develop a regular method of intercommunication. The most desirable arrangement would be for the supervisor of the community unit to attend the superintendent's staff meeting. The Inmate Advisory Council, a regularly scheduled body to aid in inmate-staff communication, could also be helpful. However, although the over-all integrity of the institution must not be jeopardized, the relationships of the community with other units in the institution must not be permitted to interfere with its separate identity.

These factors are important for the development of group cohesiveness and for the growth of responsibility and mutual concern among the inmate members of the unit.

In going to some length in discussing the significance of the location and its interrelatedness to other institution units, we may seem to have taken a theoretical position. Actually, the problem is immediate and practical. If the supervisor of the correctional community is insecure, is threatened by his colleagues, he will be unable to manage this demanding program effectively. On the other hand, if he has a good understanding of the principles of the correctional community, has reasonable freedom in his latitude of operations, has an open mind to suggestions from inmates and staff members of the unit, then there is a much more satisfactory psychological environment for the development of the correctional-community program. Keeping his colleagues informed of what he is trying to do will facilitate the acceptance of the program in the institution.

The size of the unit is limited by the ability of the inmates and staff to communicate and observe effectively the interaction taking place. This means a unit which provides adequate opportunity for behavior to be noted, analyzed, and communicated by those in the group. An important practical factor limiting the effective size of the correctional community is the acoustics of the room used for the large-group meeting. It is obvious that everyone should be able to hear clearly what is being said. Another possible limiting factor is seating arrangements. Everyone in the group should be able to see everybody else. The most convenient arrangement is seating in a circle; however, there is a limit to its size. If a correctional community is being established in a dormitory of fifty beds, it is suggested that the project begin with fifteen or twenty inmates selected on the basis of some evidence of interest and maturity. A smaller group is more manageable and at the same time gives the staff an opportunity to establish the methods of operation.

After the first few sessions the group could be increased so that within a few weeks the entire quota of fifty inmates could be incorporated harmoniously and without seriously upsetting the climate which had been established. Moreover, the staff would by this time, have enough rapport with the initial group to gain their cooperation in helping the new member inmates to adjust.

There were eighty inmates in one of the early correctional communities in a forestry camp. The size of the community and the isolated location were favorable for the introduction of the program. At the camp a high degree of interdependence was necessary, and the successful functioning of the community was therefore stressed. Acts of carelessness, shirking, inconsiderateness, abuses of privileges, thievery, temper flare-ups, or any violations of rules were likely to affect the individuals, and all members assigned to the camp. Thus, in this forestry camp, everyone had a stake in seeing that emotional outbursts or violations of the rules of conduct were brought out for serious study by the inmates and staff in the large- or small-group meetings.

The weekly schedule was determined by the community supervisor and his staff. The entire community, including all inmates, the forestry supervisors, and the staff met daily in a large-group meeting lasting forty minutes. This was followed by meetings of small groups. Four of the small groups were composed of 16-man forestry crews, and the fifth of inmates who performed clerical and maintenance work at camp headquarters. The large or community meetings were followed by reviews or seminars attended only by the staff.

The California Rehabilitation Center at Corona houses 1,800 male narcotics addicts. The institution is divided into 60-bed dormitories, each of which is a separate correctional community. Correctional communities in units of 100 men are considered by some workers to be too large for good communication, although it has been claimed that they were effective. There have been unpublished reports of favorable effects from housing units as large as 300 when subdivided into smaller units of 75 or 150 each.

THE SELECTION OF INMATES

If the staff has sufficient skill and patience the correctional community could probably be introduced into any institution. We believe that inmates in many kinds of correctional institutions would be responsive to this type of program; just how large a proportion of them is still open for study. However, due to the conservative and change-resisting nature of correctional institutions, most correctional communities have been started cautiously in one or two housing units. At first, only the more amenable and mature inmates have been invited to join the program. Other criteria of selection have been used, such as age, social background, type of offense, and especially willingness to join. Sometimes before inmates are admitted, they have been required to sign an agreement which defines the conditions of their participation in the correctional community. These precautions in choosing inmates for the therapeutic community have been thought necessary to establish the atmosphere in which the community could function successfully. After the staff have acquired experience, developed skills, and learned to function in their new community roles, and after the program has become a part of the institutional culture, a more liberalized sampling of inmates may be in order.

The following procedures and sources of information or referral have been used in selecting inmates for the unit:

Screening of institutional case files, especially of new arrivals,

Referrals from interested employees or members of the paroling authority,

Soliciting inmate volunteers through the institutional newspaper or bulletin boards,

Referral by the institutional Classification or Disciplinary committees,

Selection by objective criteria, such as standard personality tests or inventories, or a Base-Expectancy Rating Scale,

Recruitment in other institutions, including arrangements for transfers of those selected.

The selection process includes a screening of the candidate conducted by members of the staff. The process of screening applicants may begin with a group meeting of the candidates. A brief description of the unit and its purposes may first be given. The candidates are then told that admission is by request only but that because of limitations of space and other reasons not all who apply can be accepted. Thereafter, the individual screening interviews are conducted. The staff member who conducts these sessions may have the candidate's file before him. After the candidate leaves, the criteria for admission are used by the screening committee in the actual process of selection. Inmates who are not accepted are notified.

The more mature inmate members may be asked by the staff to assist at these interviews. In this way they have the experience of rendering a service to the program, and an opportunity to assume a responsible role in the unit. The effects upon the candidate of having one of his peers participate in his selection are impressive. It is a realistic introduction of the candidates to the strikingly different roles which inmates take in the correctional community.

LENGTH OF STAY

The length of participation of an inmate in the correctional community depends on several factors. His readiness for treatment is one. His capacity to enter freely into discussions and to talk in the group about things of a threatening nature to himself are important. Ordinarily, because of the unfamiliar nature of the program, it takes time for individuals to engage in and to profit from the program; for example, many men are troubled and even confused for a time by the confrontations in the group sessions. Those who do not adjust to a group situation may need to stay longer. The desirable minimal length of time in the community is six months. However, men have profited from shorter stays.

What criteria should be used to determine when a man has accomplished what he needs and should be released from the community? Some men are permitted to leave who appear to have made advances toward greater maturity and seem ready to profit from the other kinds of experiences in the institution. Inmates may be released who cannot sustain the improvement. These need to be interviewed to determine whether they would benefit by being returned to the correctional community. On the other hand, some men have progressed so remarkably that they become unusually skilled in helping their fellow inmates in the community.

THE USE OF ANECDOTAL REPORTS

The new and complex development of correctional communities may be illustrated by a description of real events. The following accounts or "anecdotal reports" refer to incidents or developments in different types of units. In Anecdotal Reports 1 and 2, for example, the difference between the viewpoint in the administration of the correctional community and conventional administrative practices is notable. These actual occurrences may help in the understanding of the correctional community because they convey the emotional climate in a community—they are accounts of feelings rather than intellectual information.

The following incident, freely edited from a mimeographed report by Campbell (6), occurred when a group was still resisting the purposes of the correctional community:

ANECDOTAL REPORT 1: Handling Problems of Stealing and Contraband

The Location. — In the community dormitory of a large institution, there were sixty inmates who had been convicted of offenses concerning the use or sale of narcotics. The unit had been in existence several months during which there had been many changes in personnel. It had an unusually rapid inmate turnover. The average stay of an inmate in the unit was four months. As an example of the operation of the correctional community, the group was a poor one. The inmates had functioned largely defensively. They had avoided their problems. They resorted to manipulation when it served their purposes. In short, they had not "congealed" as a group.

The staff had discussed the importance of their future well-being of what they might gain from the correctional community, and how it could help them to overcome their weaknesses through what would be gained from accepting responsibility for their own behavior and from becoming aware of the needs of others in the community and trying to help them.

The Incident. — A jar of maple syrup was reported missing from a truck on which a crew had been working. Search revealed that some other items, including two jars of contraband tomato juice were also missing. These matters were brought up in the community group. The confrontation had good results with all but one of the individuals involved in bringing out their anxiety about their behavior. This man refused to respond initially to the questions put to him by either staff members or his peers in the group. Then he answered defensively that he would work this matter out for himself and did not want to get involved with the group. He refused to talk about his participation in the incident. Since this refusal to cooperate was a violation of the agreements that he had made when admitted to the group, his lack of cooperation was discussed by the community. They decided that he be placed in the security unit in the institution.

The Process. — In subsequent meetings of the community group, the syrup incident was declared to be the "responsibility of everyone." The staff members present asked the inmates why they allowed this incident to happen. The responses of the inmates indicated that their "inmate code" viewpoints were not consistent with those expected of a group of people trying to develop a wholesome community. Their inadequate understanding of the purposes of the correctional community was summed up by one of the inmates who said, "We're convicts. This is a prison. Every man here has his own number to do. [His own sentence to serve.]" This statement enabled the staff to discuss again the purposes of the correctional community and to explain why the "convict code" with its dictum "every man for himself," defeated its purposes. Unless the group could accept responsibility for each other, no improvement in this delinquent, inmate culture could be expected. The point was made that the "convict culture" was interfering with whatever treatment might be expected in the community. Its influence on the behavior of the group was disturbing the initial progress toward greater community-centered responsibility that had been made in previous weeks.

Several inmates were aware that this incident was their attempt to center responsibility for the life of the community in the individual rather than the community. Other outspoken members stated that they recognized the need for greater concern by everyone in the community for the behavior of its individual members. However, they recognized that it was not possible to take any of the necessary steps in this direction as long as the antisocial climate continued to exist.

These statements encouraged the staff to renewed efforts to bring about a change. They decided that it was up to the group to resolve the seeming impasse created in the group by the "convict culture." In other words, the burden for doing something about the situation was given to the group. At first there was some resistance, some questioning why this was being done to them. Some even saw this as a form of punishment. The staff maintained that it was up to the group to work through this impasse and that it required an unusual effort for them. Gradually the group responded to the challenge. One of their first actions was to form a voluntary evening group. The first meetings were characterized by a sense of confusion and aimlessness as they tried to reconcile their differences. Some refused to become involved. However, the enthusiasm and determination of some members increased with widening participation until almost the total population of the barracks participated.

Now the group began to express concern for the man who had been placed in the security unit. A delegation of three was authorized to visit him. They reported to the group that he now saw his responses differently and desired to return to the barracks. They pointed out that the community was anxious to work with him and recommended that he be returned. Upon his return, no immediate significant change was noted. Then an incident occurred that revealed the attitudes of the group.

Another Problem Arises and Is Resolved. — Another man in the group was discovered to have a contraband article, an unauthorized set of earphones. The man himself brought his offense to the attention of the group. As the group discussed the situation, they arrived at the opinion that his action was a manifestation of his need for immediate gratification of any desire. The group was at a loss as to what to do. At this point the staff pointed out the need "for the group" to do something to the inmate; because of his behavior, the implication was punishment. The inmates said he had been punished many times before without effect. They felt that they should express concern for his well-being, not punishment. The staff maintained that something should be done more than talk to force the man to face the implications of his actions. This was recommended in terms of inmate morale, and in terms of the consequences of the repetition of this type of compulsive behavior on parole. The community group decided to assign him as punishment *extra duty* in the form of mowing the large barrack area grass. When asked how he felt about this, the inmate questioned the group's sincerity. He said that the staff caused him to be punished, and criticized the inmates for letting themselves be manipulated. It became evident that his comments had a considerable impact on the inmates.

The next afternoon when he began to mow the lawn, the men in the group volunteered to help him. In later discussions in the large group, they acknowledged that they did this to demonstrate their own responsibility for his misconduct. They also wanted him to know that they were concerned for him and not merely following the suggestion for his punishment made by the staff. They were also expiating their sense of guilt because they had in fact agreed with the staff.

The Group Concern with the Man of the Earlier Incident. — The same afternoon that the lawn was being mowed cooperatively, the man who had stolen the maple syrup and had been released from the security unit was interviewed by his field parole agent. The agent reported that the man was upset and depressed. He asked to be removed from the community living program and transferred to another institution. The men in the group were concerned when they heard this. Unknown to the staff, a special group meeting was called that evening. No record was made of that meeting, but it had a dramatic effect upon this man.

The next morning he opened the discussion in the group, speaking confidently and with determination. The staff was surprised and wanted to know what had taken place. The men had appointed him temporary spokesman for the large-group session. This acceptance of him and respect for him had changed him. The community, without the assistance of the staff, had changed his emotional state and given him a real role in the community group.

The Meaning of These Incidents. — The events in the lives of these two inmates are examples of the treatment potential in prison inmates. Their sensitivity and perception of each other's needs had helped to influence their peers. This is possible when they feel secure, can set aside suspicion, hostility, and resentment to authority. These two men felt more strength to face problems and to do something about them because of the acceptance and assistance of the group. More important was the fact that the group, in its special evening session, had decided on their own that they wanted a chance to try to manage their own affairs; they no longer were content to be dependent and helpless. They next drew up a set of "house rules" governing behavior in the community. They recommended that any infraction of these rules would be discussed in special evening groups. The "evening groups" were an attempt to escape the belittling effects of the staff's leading them. Whatever disciplinary action they recommended would be brought to the attention of the staff daily in the regularly scheduled morning community groups. They felt that the community group could be used more constructively to help them understand delinquent behavior.

The staff was encouraged by their conduct. The inmate group had accepted the idea that they must think about their "here-and-now" behavior in the dormitory. When they felt inclined to commit some offenses, they were expected to discuss them in the large group. They became optimistic about being able to develop mature ways of considering their behavior in advance of committing delinquent acts. Thus they hopefully would grow toward more mature ways of conducting themselves in the daily life of the institutional community and afterwards on parole.

HOW THE DILEMMA OF CUSTODY AND TREATMENT IS MET

Traditionally, correctional institutions divide the responsibilities of institutional management into custodial and treatment divisions. This dichotomy is "institutionalized" by having two separate and parallel lines of prison administration and staff promotion. The employees identify with one or the other of these roles in institutional operation and isolate themselves from the other. In contrast to this, a major objective in the model correctional community is that *these two functions, custody and treatment, are combined in the activities of all staff members.*

The staff of the correctional community must understand that the old-time division of responsibility is abolished in the correctional community. Everyone on the staff has a responsibility for the total orderly operation of the unit. Everyone on the staff has a responsibility to be familiar with the nature and purposes of training and treatment and to cooperate in their accomplishment. Every member of the staff is part of the team to carry out the overall objectives of the program.

In some places, the title "program administrator" is used for the supervisor. His job combines both custodial and treatment functions. The employees in the correctional community are organized as a staff team. In the housing unit, the staff team consists of teachers, correctional officers, correctional counselors, and others. There is some participation in each other's operations. For example, the dormitory supervisor might carry a caseload under the supervision of the correctional counselor and be involved in some of the casework or classification activities. The correctional counselor might supervise a cottage or dormitory group, while the dormitory officer conducts a small group.

THE MEANING OF AUTHORITY IN THE
CORRECTIONAL COMMUNITY

Inmates and employees in the ordinary correctional institution are accustomed to the traditional use of authority. For the ordinary cell block in a prison or a dormitory in a juvenile institution, explicit rules and regulations determine its operation. They state what can and what cannot be done. The inmates generally know when authorities will intervene and enforce regulations. As illustrated by Anecdotal Report 1, the correctional community is different.

Some rules of correctional institutions occasionally have to be waived in the correctional community to further the inmates' responsibility. Dr. Harry Wilmer has stated this point of view with regard to the government of the correctional community and the responsibilities of the supervisor, others on the staff, and the inmates (37, p. 13): "While he (the supervisor) is ready to lend the community his professional skills, the community is not to expect him to solve by administrative fiat, *ex cathedra* pronouncements, or punitive disciplinary measures those of its problems which are created for it by its own unruly members." What Wilmer points out is illustrated in the second anecdotal report, following below, where the inmate group solved the problems created by its own unruly members.

In view of the realities of institutional management, some limitations must be enforced with regard to the activities of the inmate participants in the correctional community. They are members of a large society and must live within the dictates of that society. Necessary rules against attempts to escape, felonious behavior, and physical attacks upon staff or inmates, must be enforced. However, some everyday operations within the community, such as the control of TV and radio may be conveniently left to the inmate group to decide. In such matters, the rules of social conduct in the correctional community differ little from those likely to be found in outside groups.

Departmental rules and regulations apply to the community. However, the methods of handling violations in the correctional community may vary somewhat from traditional ones. There are differences of opinion as to how far correctional communities may go in dealing with these violations. The latitude extended is determined by the total of the institutional traditions and operations. In the ideal correctional community it may be possible to explore candidly the totality of a violation and its report in the correctional community. How minor violations may be handled through group discussion and decisions is illustrated in Anecdotal Report 2.

After disciplinary reports are processed in this way, they are sent through routine channels to the administrative offices of the institution. The recommendations may be modified by higher-ranking officials or, when necessary, the case may be referred to the institutional disciplinary committee. What happens in these routine channels should be discussed in the community. The sharing of authority, the accomplishment of some socially desirable mean between license and repression, must be accomplished by the cooperation of both inmates and staff. For, as Wilmer points out (37, p. 70): "Freedom in the therapeutic community was never synonymous with laissez-faire.

There were definite limits on behavior. Freedom to be ill or frightened is one thing; freedom to run away and retreat from society is another. The essence of the analytic situation is that the patient is free to feel and free to put these feelings into words. He is not, however, free to act except within the confines of the formal analytic role expected of him. Freedom is thus a relative concept just as permissiveness is. Any attempt to be absolute on these matters is as arbitrary as full discipline and repression."

In the correctional community, occasional defiance or even delinquent behavior is an inevitable price to pay in the process of inmate maturation. The staff should bring incidents of hostility before the inmates. Unless they can see the meaning of their behavior, they cannot mature. In a book written more than three decades ago Aichhorn (1) describes how the maturity of juvenile delinquents seemed to parallel their freedom to express destructive hostility upon institutional property. An illustrative incident reported by Briggs and Dowling (4) occurred in a correctional community for fifty young adult inmates. They were housed in an open dormitory building in a minimum-custody, adult correctional institution.

ANECDOTAL REPORT 2: Hostility During a Change in Leadership

In the early stages of the "Pine Hall Project," the supervisor attended all daily meetings and devoted himself to other activities, even at times when he was not on duty. He felt that this personal attention was important to establish the new culture in which continuous treatment could take place. During this time, progress was made toward the establishment of an effective correctional community. At the end of the first six months of the project, the supervisor had to be away for the first time since it began. In order to try to prepare the group for his absence, he announced a few days in advance that he would be leaving in a week on a business trip and designated another staff member who would act for him during his absence.

Temporary Change of Leadership. — At the first community meeting after he had gone, the temporary supervisor, perhaps because of his insecurity in assuming leadership, and even perhaps because

of doubts about the program, opened the community group by
confirming that he would be in charge of the project during the
absence of the regular supervisor. Apparently the way he made
this announcement made the men anxious. The supervisor's leaving
may have promoted feelings that they had been rejected. The
supervisor, moreover, had left them in the hands of an insecure
and skeptical substitute.

The project was not yet securely established. At the end of this
large group session, the acting leader summarized the session by
saying that, so far as he was concerned, there was still "a line of
difference or separation between inmates and staff." Since some of
the inmates had begun tentatively to share the responsibility of
some staff roles, the supervisor's skepticism seemed like a reprimand.
Some inmates refused to leave the large-group meeting, but the
acting leader and his small-group members left. The community
was thus split into two factions, those who had refused to leave
and those who left. At their earnest request, the substitute leader
returned to the large group. However, the troubled feelings were
not dissipated. All community members seemed disturbed by the
turn of events.

The Process. – During the next few days, windows were broken,
beds were not made; the unit was in a very disordered state in
contrast to its previous orderliness. When the supervisor returned,
he saw the broken windows and the general disorderliness. Even
though he had been back only a few minutes, inmates began to
chastise him for not having the windows repaired, etc. He was
called an inadequate supervisor, and that he ought to get on the
job at once since the room was drafty due to the broken windows.
The supervisor stated that the windows should not be replaced
until it was discovered why they had been broken. This was the
topic discussed during several days in the large group.

Meanwhile, there were administrative pressures to have the
windows replaced; institutional glaziers had come and been sent
away without repairing the damage. The supervisor was determined
to give the community the opportunity to face the disturbed situation. Finally, after the fourth group meeting the men were able
to confess that they had been annoyed with him for leaving. One
inmate began to take him to task personally, saying, "If you're such
a big shot making trips to headquarters, why don't you just stay
away from here?" And they went on and pointed out other inadequacies that they felt he had. On the fifth day, they were able to

say that they had missed him, and that they had felt lost, alone, and unsure because of the acting supervisor's attitudes. They also felt that the project was under fire and that they were now at the mercy of skeptics on the institutional staff in high administrative positions.

Discussion of the Above Events. — This incident illustrates how disorder can be understood and worked through the group itself rather than handled according to the usual rules and regulations in correctional institutions. If the administrative arrangements had not been clearly defined before the program began, the operation of the correctional community would have been jeopardized. The glazier's art would have prevailed over the search for the psychological meaning of the broken windows. In this instance the group itself was able gradually to understand its own behavior and to work through the emotional events.

It is through these periods of destructive behavior that growth may come about in the group. If the top administrator had reacted by suddenly ordering the unit to "clear up the mess," the whole purpose of therapy in the correctional community might have been lost. The amount of money needed in repairing the damage was minor. However, some staff members are comfortable with traditional concepts of institutional management and see only the broken windows and unmade beds, and not the reasons. The higher officials in this incident were confident that the disorder would be overcome and that something constructive for the inmates' growth would eventuate. In short, they had confidence in the persons they had selected to conduct the correctional community. In consequence mutual respect and trust grew between institutional administration and correctional community.

QUALIFICATIONS AND RECRUITMENT OF THE STAFF

The importance of the personal qualities of the staff members, who together with the inmate population determine the success of the program. The staff should have the following personal qualifications:

A belief in the possibilities of change for the better in inmates.

Patience and optimism, a sense of humor, the ability to work with others, a good memory, and the capacity to accept understandingly and not be threatened by the hostility and unreasonableness of the inmates and sometimes of skeptical colleagues.

The capacity to wait for an increase in maturity in the group rather than having a need to get results by forcing inmates to do what seems desirable for their own welfare.

The ability to share responsibility with the inmate group.

Willingness to do extra duty and to expend the time needed for further professional study.

When the correctional-community program is about to start, notices should circulate in the institution to announce the recruitment of the first-line staff. Subsequently, applicants should be invited to visit the unit. The supervisor of the unit should interview all applicants. If later some of these are found not to be acceptable, they should be notified of the decision and told of the staff's appreciation of their interest. Because of the demands that the community makes upon the staff, appointments may be made on a thirty-day trial basis. During this period, some employees find that they are not patient enough to work with a particular group. They become tense when the group does not move quickly toward the solution of a problem, or takes no action. If it is necessary to release employees from the unit, they should be seen by the supervisor and the reasons for transfer discussed with them.

In the selection of the supervisor of a correctional community, the question has been raised whether he must have some "rare" personal qualities. One could list many desirable traits which would include a number of human virtues. However, supervisors need not have "rare" personal qualities. Experience with correctional communities has borne out the fact that the effect upon the correctional community is not fatal when a gifted leader is replaced by someone else.

Problems will inevitably arise whenever there is a change in leadership. To diminish disruptiveness it is desirable for the new leader to work in the community for a time with the one who is leaving. In this way the future leader becomes familiar with his predecessors' points of view and methods. This

facilitates the transition and reduces the likelihood of disturbances or manipulations. It is also less disturbing to others on
the staff who do not have to face the sudden innovations of
working with an unfamiliar leader. The goal in changing supervisors is to minimize the feelings of loss, separation, and rejection, and maximize the continuity of the group and recognize
and encourage its ability to accept a new staff member.

Other valuable members of the staff team are clinical psychologists and psychiatric social workers. They should be selected
for their skill in working with staff members individually and
for their capacity to contribute meaningful analyses and suggestions during the groups and the post-sessions. These clinically trained persons are valuable as objective interpreters of
the correctional community process. When the group takes a
seemingly inexplicable turn, the clinically trained team member should be able to clarify the situation. In times of disappointment or in the presence of doubts or misgivings, the
clinician may give the necessary insight to renew the enthusiasm of the staff for the program.

In addition to the full-time clinical staff members, California
institutions employ part-time services of outside consultants in
psychiatry, clinical psychology, and social work. The frequency
and length of their visits should be enough to provide these
clinicians with an accurate picture of the unit. Ideally, they
should come weekly and participate in the groups. Consultants
have served as advisors to the correctional community and assisted in staff-training. They have contributed to seminars and
round-table discussions as a part of the in-service training program. Their usefulness is increased when they put their observations concerning the progress of the unit in writing and
indicate areas they have noted.

The role of the consultant should, however, be only advisory. Regardless of how strongly he may disagree with the
program and may want to interfere in the operation, he should
never assume administrative control of the unit. A good consultant must be competent in both theory and practice. He
must have the skill to make his opinions and advice clear and

yet to do so without being offensive. Because the role of consultants is so demanding, their selection and recruitment present many difficulties.

SPECIAL DEMANDS UPON THE CORRECTIONAL COMMUNITY STAFF

The ordinary correctional institution must be conservative. Experience has shown that some of the most enthusiastically heralded and promising innovations in prisons and reformatories have led to disappointment and unfortunate consequences for the inmates, the staff, and departmental officials. Consequently, the employees entering a correctional community must be forewarned that the road ahead is not smooth and easy. The staff of the correctional community in a large institution may be subjected to skeptical and critical attitudes from their colleagues. Moreover, some colleagues may believe that jobs in the special unit are easier for the staff and also provide special advantages for promotion. Hence, in addition to the normal and expected resistance to something new in a conservative agency, the staff of the unit may also be troubled by what seems like jealous or resentful attitudes in some of their colleagues.

The employee in a community must be prepared to work extra hours because of the unconventional schedule and unique procedures in the correctional community. Initially, he may feel exploited, but in the long run he may become a dedicated worker in the correctional community. The interesting and intriguing problems of the correctional community cannot be left behind when it is time to go home.

With a series of relationship failures behind them, inmates often look at the good will and interest of the employee with suspicion and distrust. Instead of obtaining appreciation for his labor and consideration, the staff member may be subjected to hostile criticisms from the inmates he is trying to help.

A dormitory established as a correctional community may be regarded as a favored unit. When other dormitories in the same institution must conform with the details of departmental regulations and the correctional community is allowed to deviate from some of these customary rules, the issue of favoritism arises. For example, in the early morning, while their colleagues are carrying on the regular work or training programs, the staff of the correctional community spend an hour or more in group discussion. Again, if the inmates in the correctional community are permitted to watch television later at night than the other dormitories, or the staff engage in competitive games with them or otherwise seem to "fraternize" with the inmates, then the community unit is viewed as a privileged place for the inmates in comparison with the rest of the institution. If the staff of the correctional community may choose whether or not to wear uniforms, this may give them a favored status and affect their relationships with their colleagues.

Employees outside the program may be concerned when the titles and activities of the community employees are different from those of other employees of similar rank. Other sources of irritation to their colleagues were the overtime without pay put in by the enthusiastic staff members of the community unit. This is a justifiably threatening development in terms of civil-service practice and needs to be considered carefully by institutional administrators. The different status of the correctional community imposes a responsibility upon the staff members to help other employees to become better informed about its operations.

For adequate in-service training it is imperative, upon introduction of the correctional community, to give full opportunity to the entire staff of the institution to learn about the program. This should be done, aside from lectures and discussions, by giving them first-hand, on-the-job experience in the program. The values of this combination of theory and practice in the advancement of the correctional-community program in several youth and adult correctional institutions has been reported in a recent publication (11) describing such a training program in the development of institutional treatment programs. In-service training must be planned to bring to the attention of everyone in the institution the potential values in greater job satisfaction and improved status for all of them when the correctional-community program has been successful.

GLYNN B. SMITH

THE NATURE AND FUNCTIONS
OF THE COMMUNITY GROUP

THE ATMOSPHERE IN THE COMMUNITY GROUP

The large community group is new in correctional practice. An adequate understanding of the large-group process requires an opportunity to observe a successful community group in action.

The purpose of the community group is to develop a constructive atmosphere of mutual helpfulness among those in the group. By "constructive" we mean an atmosphere assisting growth toward maturity of its members. By contrast, the inmate code or delinquent social system is destructive, particularly upon the less mature inmates in the group. A constructive atmosphere in the large group is achieved under the following conditions:

Inmates and staff accept each other *as persons* and are concerned about each other's welfare.

Discussions are conducted in a nonjudgmental climate. Behavior is looked at and discussed without judging, so far as possible, whether it is good or bad, right or wrong. This does not, however, imply acceptance or approval. The goal of the large group is not to condone delinquent acts. The members should assume nonjudgmental attitudes to advance self-awareness and avoid defensiveness or projection of blame.

The group seeks to develop each individual's ability to understand how others feel about him, and why they have these feelings.

Members of the group learn that to help oneself it is necessary to want to be helpful toward others in the group.

THE GOALS OF THE COMMUNITY GROUP

These conditions create the desired atmosphere of the large or community group. If the supervisor, his staff, and the inmates are successful in achieving them, inmate social growth can occur.

As a correctional community matures, it discards much of the delinquent culture and assumes greater responsibility. The level of maturity of the correctional community depends on the following factors:

A change from submission to the inmate culture to acceptance of help from the treatment program offered by the staff and inmates.

The aid given by inmates and staff to the group members in developing meaningful, constructive, interpersonal relationships.

The learning ability of the inmates to differentiate feelings from behavior, and to understand how feelings affect behavior.

The help given to inmates from their peers in learning about themselves and their behavior. The group focuses on real observed behavior, and their frank appraisal enables inmates to profit from their mistakes and to meet crises, problems, and tensions of daily institutional living. This understanding of strengths and weaknesses helps toward greater maturity. Through these gains in self-knowledge, provided by the group, better self-control is developed by the inmates for handling the stresses and temptations in their lives. The group culture facilitates the inmate's growth in capacity to assume responsibilities.

GUIDELINES FOR THE BEGINNING STAFF MEMBER

An initial explanation of the goals of the community group to the inmates is probably neither possible nor desirable. This would be as difficult as trying to explain swimming to a person who had never seen anyone swimming. The goals must be communicated to the inmates by the staff's behavior and participation in the community groups, and by the inmate's involvement in the process.

Caution in Participation. — The new staff member should begin by being a careful, attentive observer rather than an active participant during his first large-group meetings. At first, he should abstain from any lengthy statements in the large group. He should not participate in group discussions despite urging from the inmates. There are no rules for staff response, but there are some guidelines: Staff response should be based entirely upon their diagnosis of the group's status at the moment, and in relation to the purpose and goals of the community. It takes time and experience to be able to do this and for this reason the new staff member is encouraged to be a good listener and observer. For example, at times the counselor may respond to a question by asking if anyone else in the group could help this person. At other times, when it is obvious that a ridiculous or manipulative question has been asked, the counselor may respond with silence and allow inmate members to handle the situation. The counselor may respond to a question with another question if he is attempting to determine what is transpiring. Anecdotal Report 3 illustrates how a capable staff handles troublesome inmate inquiries.

ANECDOTAL REPORT 3: Much Ado about a Dormitory Shakedown

The Disturbing Incident. — The Supervisor, Mr. A., was in charge of a 60-man correctional community in a dormitory in a large institution. For ten weeks he had met with them in the large group. One morning, as he entered the meeting room, he felt tension in the air. The meeting was opened by several individuals who reported that during the previous day, between late afternoon and midnight, the lockers of all residents had been searched by the dormitory officer.

Mr. A. listened to their indignation even as they stated that they understood the need for the search. They did not complain about the search itself but about the manner in which it was done: after searching their lockers, their beds were rumpled and their personal possessions carelessly tossed about. For approximately twenty minutes they poured out their feelings of criticism of the officer. They thought that correctional officers should be selected carefully to eliminate those with sadistic trends, and that this correctional officer "should be fired."

Mr. A. did not respond, so the inmates attempted to manipulate a response. One of them said, "Mr. A., we know that you are interested in helping us, but all of your efforts are being flushed down the drain in the evening when this correctional officer treats us this way." Still the counselor did not respond, so a more aggressive method was used. Injustices were listed. Another inmate asked: "Mr. A., is it fair the way this correctional officer treated us?"

Mr. A. was trying to evaluate what was taking place in the group. The issue was not whether the correctional officer had been fair or not; it was clear that in their eyes he was cruel.

Mr. A. recognized the inmates' approach as an attempt to manipulate him to take sides. He tried to help the group members look at what was going on, so he said: "You asked me, 'Were the correctional officer's actions fair?' If I answer the question by saying 'yes,' what does it mean? If, on the other hand, I answer by saying 'no,' what does this mean? As a group, what do you think you are really trying to do?" This comment stopped the hostility, and brought out a laugh as if he caught on or "found them out." Some had not been fully aware of the manipulation. Others, who felt their efforts had been skillfully disguised, admired the way in which Mr. A. had confronted them with the issue and did not allow himself to be trapped.

In dealing with a direct and pointed question which he feels he must or should answer, the new staff member should give a brief, straight-forward reply. Even if the question is an embarrassing one, he should avoid the normal tendency to get himself out of an uncomfortable situation.

Relate to the individual as part of the group. — There is a tendency for new staff leaders to relate to individuals within the community rather than to the community itself. That is, they talk to one person at a time in the group, almost oblivious to the effect of their verbal response on the other members of the group. Also, they are less observant of nonverbal communications and have no idea of what has transpired in the group other than their own interaction with the one person. It is important for staff to realize that what they say to one member of the community is also communicated to all others present.

Therefore, it is important not to relate a person as an individual but to him as a part of the community group.

Restraint in the use of rules and structure. — There are few general rules for the operation of the large group. Each community group establishes its own operational procedures, rules, and customs. The rules may differ from community to community depending upon the inmate and the leader. When a group is started, it is desirable to allow the inmates latitude to develop reasonable rules.

When staff members become anxious and attempt to provide detailed structure for the conduct of the group, they inhibit development of inmate responsibility, and inmates should accept the responsibility for the conduct of the large group as soon as possible. When such responsibility is given to inmates, there is always the possibility that some will seek to manipulate to get their own way. Although the staff should allow the inmates leeway in the community to make mistakes and to learn from them, the staff must never overlook that the control of the group cannot be delegated to the inmates.

Experience indicates that the correctional-community approach will ultimately bring about better management, but this does not mean a smooth-unit operation without tensions or problems. To the contrary, the staff must allow the community latitude to make mistakes within limits and to learn from them. In addition, the staff must handle their own anxieties when inmates begin to complain about conditions and about staff behavior. This is the group's initial but feeble effort to develop some order out of what seems to them chaos.

Another way of viewing group development is noted by Dr. Paul Sivadon, a French psychiatrist, who reported on the techniques of sociotherapy. He based his approach on the staff encouraging the group and individual inmates to protest against their environment. Sivadon (28) stated that this facilitates the mobilization of energy of the participants and promotes the cohesiveness of the group so that it ultimately arrives at the point where the individuals work together person to person. When the staff members do not attempt to suppress the opposition, they are, to some extent, included in the group. Sivadon sees the group members express themselves first in opposition, next in aggressiveness, followed by activity, and finally in creation.

In the large group, opposition and aggressiveness can be expressed in words rather than actions. This aggressiveness expressed in words can be channeled into creativeness and acceptance. The large community group can provide a time and place for this needed expression. If there is a sincere effort by the staff to understand this expression, the energy can be channeled constructively. Sivadon stated: "To the extent that the patient does not oppose the situation of being hospitalized, he has a tendency to be satisfied with his state of being sick, and the chances of recovery are compromised. On the other hand, if he opposes his situation, and if this opposition is not utilized therapeutically, it will be expressed by the refusal of treatment or even by escape or violence" (28).

This indicates the importance of the community-group meeting as a place for the encouragement of this expression.

The concept of minimal structure and direction in helping the group members work through their developmental problems can be viewed from the stated framework. Frequently, when the group attempts to provide rigid structure, such as Rules of Order, an elected chairman, a prepared agenda before each group, this effort will be made through a steamroller technique which does not consider the total group's desires. When the staff leader is skillfully able to question why this structure is necessary, or if the majority of the group really want the structure, the steamrolling, which does not consider the feelings of all, begins to bog down. This leaves the group in a state of uncertainty, and they begin as a group to become, as stated by Dr. Sivadon, opposed to their group situation.

The aggressiveness motivated by a person's opposition to his predicament is often expressed by criticism of the group leader, or possibly by a desperate attempt to use the steamroller maneuver to get one's own way. For example, the alternative may be presented by stating: "All those in favor of electing a chairman or accepting agenda, raise their hands." When the staff leader questions why a vote is necessary, hostility is expressed by saying: "After all, this is the democratic way, the American way." An effort must then be made to help the group recognize that voting satisfies the majority but ignores or thrusts aside the minority. This lack of concern for others is the very thing that the inmates must understand; that is, how does a group resolve a problem considering *all* involved instead of the few aggressive verbal individuals. This effort may require several group meetings.

The demand for structure to feel comfortable comes from an aggressive minority, although initially it would appear different during the steamroller effort. The real group activity then becomes evident as the group slowly establishes structure. At this juncture, a more mature level of operation is usually achieved. An accepting and understanding atmosphere is beginning in which all persons can ultimately be heard and have their needs considered.

SPECIFIC PROBLEMS FACING THE BEGINNER
IN THE COMMUNITY GROUP

The beginner will naturally have some doubt as to his role when he first attends a large-group meeting. Unless he has experience in group-counseling, the meeting may be so unusual that he may not know what to say or how to behave during the first session. The beginner should remain silent so far as possible. We will now consider the three problems which inexperienced staff members often meet:

1. The Large Group Arouses Anxiety

A new staff member will become anxious in his first large group meeting and may react unwisely when inmates are hostile or indifferent. He should try a method, described in detail later, of observation of the "content" or words and "process" or group messages. Anecdotal Report 3 illustrates how an experienced staff member realized what was going on and by a frank summary of the situation guided the large group toward a constructive development.

2. Staff Member Need Not Justify What He Says

Even though a new staff member feels his position to be absolutely right, he should avoid being drawn into an argument. The correctional community functions best when the inmates themselves arrive at the solution of a problem or the answer to a question.

The need to defend or justify one's actions is greatest when one is actually wrong or is wrongly accused. A staff member is unwise if he tries to argue himself out of such a situation or tries to evade facing facts in a large group. In other words, his behavior differs from the inmate's behavior, and so he is a person with whom they can identify in their search for maturity. This type of situation is illustrated in Anecdotal Report 4, in which a staff member frankly admits an error. He was thereafter seen as a more competent and dependable authority figure in the eyes of the inmates.

ANECDOTAL REPORT 4: A Staff Member Faces His Own Error

The Situation. — A staff member came to the supervisor of a dormitory correctional community quite upset because he found himself in an untenable position of his own making.

An inmate had come to him "in confidence" and explained that he was scared of another inmate from a nearby dormitory community because of something that had happened between them outside the prison.

Unfortunately, the staff member did not encourage the inmate to bring the problem to the large group. The possibility of a serious incident was brewing. Since the staff member accepted the information in confidence, he felt he could not bring the problem to the group. However, he talked the matter over, in general terms, with a few inmates in the dormitory. The staff member told them the name of the inmate, and he was promptly accused of "snitching" or "ratting" on an inmate. When communication is not open and "confidences" are accepted by the staff, rumors and accusations occur.

Staff Member's Dilemma. — In the large-group meeting, where the inmates considered the matter, someone asked the staff member how he had obtained his information. He was afraid to be honest. In trying to defend the inmate, he lied and stated that he had

obtained his information from other staff members. The group chal-
lenged him at once. He denied his dishonesty. The session ended,
but there was no doubt that this situation would be discussed in
the large-group meeting the following day.

After the community meeting, the guilty staff member asked
the unit supervisor for help. He was told there were two possibilities.
He could return the following day to the community group and "lie
like a trooper." If he took this approach, he would need to tell
other lies to support the first one. The supervisor added that the
counselor would have to be a very convincing liar. The second
alternative was to admit to the group the next day that he had
lied because he felt he owed it to the man who had counted on his
keeping the matter confidential; and, furthermore, that he had lied
because he was fearful that someone might be hurt if it were known
that he had "snitched."

The Outcome. — The staff member confessed at the next group
meeting that he had lied and why he had done so. To his surprise,
the group's immediate response was one of laughter and pleasure.
They told him they had known the truth all the time and were all
wondering what he would do. They were also determined to help
the inmate with his problem as responsible members of the community. They indicated that they would try to help him face his
problems in the group and not seek confidential relationships with
the staff.

3. The Initial Function Should Not Be Action-Oriented

It is a natural reaction in one's first large-group meeting to
want to do something to show the inmate one's good will. Inmates who try to use the large group to secure advantageous
changes often ask new staff members for the things the inmates
want in their daily life. By dealing with practical needs, inmates are able to keep away from deeper needs. Everyone
wants to avoid unpleasant and difficult problems. Inmates particularly avoid trying to figure out the causes of their behavior.
The inexperienced staff member must curb this need to be
liked, and avoid a show of good intentions. By resisting being
"a good Joe" he acts with mature self-restraint, and helps the
group to do the same.

The staff must patiently and repeatedly show the inmates
that the large group is not the place to initiate immediate

changes in the operation of the institution. Things that need to be changed can be discussed, but the large group is not a forum for action and decisions. If it is the considered opinion of the large group that change is necessary, the superintendent's staff meeting or the Inmate Advisory Council should be used to effect the change. What, then, happens in these other institutional meetings should be related to the community group. This is illustrated by Anecdotal Report 3.

INTERACTIONS IN THE COMMUNITY GROUP

As soon as a staff member enters the room, he should be able to begin perceiving things which tell him about the group. Although largely nonverbal, this communication may be very meaningful. For example, when a staff leader comes in, does the group immediately become silent? Do they ignore or greet him? Do they leave it up to the supervisor to open the meeting when all are present? The answers to these questions are indications of the psychological climate of the group.

An inmate's words and actions may tell different things. He may ask the group for help to disguise his indifference and curry staff attention. When he asks, his manner may reveal a lack of sincerity. In trying to understand, we must ask: "What is this person trying to tell us? Since he knows that the supervisor is required to make a report to the parole board, is he merely putting on a good show?"

Another helpful and pointed question for a staff leader to ask himself when he is uncertain of the meaning of the group discussion is: "What is really happening here and now?" Some of the Anecdotal Reports illustrate the discrepancy between what is on the surface and what is hidden. The first step in evaluating what is actually occurring may be to ask the question, "What is the group really telling us?" For example, when the inmates are complaining about food, we should consider whether they are complaining about the lack of staff attention. There is more than one kind of nourishment. Only as staff members understand the significance of what is being communicated can they help the inmates.

An illustration of surface and hidden communications may be

cited from the discussion during a post-session following a large-group meeting at which Dr. Wilmer was a visitor. A staff member stated that when Wilmer walked in during the community meeting and sat down, he took a chair reserved for an inmate. An inmate told him bluntly and hostilely that the chair he had taken was an inmate's and that he should get himself another. In the post-session, Wilmer explained that he felt that part of what the man was saying on behalf of the group was that "visitors were not wanted, that they were intruders, especially when they came late."

It is wise to view the group on several levels of increasing complexity from the obvious here-and-now reality level to one concerned with material on the subconscious level. This last level may be most attractive to an inexperienced but psychologically informed staff member. Professional correctional workers who experience satisfaction in offering deep and theoretical interpretation of the group "process" may miss the obvious and the useful. The deep interpretations are probably the least important or fruitful, and should be discussed in a community group rarely, and then only by skilled psychotherapists.

A METHODOLOGICAL APPROACH IN APPRAISING THE COMMUNITY

A community-group meeting can be generally evaluated in terms of "content" and "process." "Content" is what is said in the group. "Process" is the total group's actions and reactions. The contents of a can of soup is soup, the process is how it is made and canned.

Not only does process refer to what is being said, but how it is being said, to whom it is being said, the gestures, and the spoken or unspoken interpersonal relationships and leadership. For example, if one were to record the interactions in terms of words alone, it might appear that the group was attempting to encourage one of their members to tell about his feelings. However, if the nonverbal communication, the accompanying gestures, facial expressions, and tones of voice of the other inmates were also taken into account, the more subtle interpretation of the process might change one's observations considerably. The group might appear to be in reality actually making an effort to get the man to keep quiet.

A method of thinking about content and process of a group which the beginner can use in practical work consists of three phases:

The investigative phase consists of observation, of asking meaningful questions to obtain information and try to determine what the problems are in the group. This is in essence the satisfaction of curiosity.

The diagnostic phase consists of studying information gathered for casual factors in the group in order to put the information to constructive use. This is a sorting or classifying of information and feelings.

The treatment phase consists, after finding the possible causes underlying the problems, of helping the group to face their problems. In this phase information and feelings are used by special group technics.

These three stages may help the inexperienced staff members to function more effectively in the large group. Sometimes, it is difficult to be patient, methodical, and orderly in the throes of an exciting session. Anecdotal Report 3 illustrates the use of these three phases.

THE STAFF SESSION AFTER
THE COMMUNITY-GROUP MEETING

An essential part of the correctional community is the post-session or staff critique that immediately follows the large-group meetings. Its purpose is to evaluate them; and it is a good method of combining staff thinking about the "content" and "process" of a group meeting. Staff critique usually lasts from fifteen minutes to an hour. When used for training, it should at least be a half hour. One important aspect of this evaluative session is the opportunity it provides for staff self-study. The staff members review what they said and did in the community group. The value of post-sessions depends upon the extent to which the staff uses them in seeking to understand honestly their activities and feelings. The following are sample questions by staff members in a good post-group session:

"Why did you go along with the inmates and say you were concerned about the service and the attitudes of the crew in the mess hall?"

"When the group was discussing an inmate's problem with his wife, why did you change the subject?"

"When the group mentioned your feelings and what you wanted to do about the problem presented by an inmate, did you recognize that you were beginning to react parentally or protectively toward him?"

For example, a staff member said to an inmate in the group: "You are becoming hostile." As a result the inmate became silent. In the post-session, other staff attempted to help this staff member recognize that his comment was due to personal anxiety and that actually it was he who was hostile to the inmate. They felt that his goal had not been to help the inmate, but to silence him because of the fear that he could not handle the inmate's hostility. This staff meeting was constructive, for the staff member recognized what he had felt and done.

By way of experimentation inmates have on occasion been permitted to attend the staff post-session meeting. This is not recommended when an institution is introducing the correctional community because the post-session periods are needed for staff training and understanding. It is difficult enough for beginning staff to look at their mistakes in the presence of their co-workers. Doing so with inmates present may prove impossible. With inmates in attendance, there is also a temptation to continue the community group itself on the subject matter which had been discussed.

The presence of a consultant, as well as the supervisor, at the post-session, provides an excellent opportunity for training. Staff development is helped by the consultant's suggestions how to feel more comfortable in the group or how to explore their reasons for feeling discomfort. For example, the staff may be shown the ways in which they are handling their own anxiety in the group. Staff might, for example, resist focusing on upsetting problem areas because of their fear of hostile reactions by inmates. Staff members may be implicitly, although perhaps not consciously, saying to the inmates: "We will not upset you if you do not upset us." The result is a stalemate in the community groups. The consultant's role in the post-session is (1) clarifying the dynamics of the group session, and (2) training the staff in understanding the meaning of staff behavior, and thereby facilitating their skills, knowledge, and effective treatment.

"FEEDBACK" OF INFORMATION TO THE
COMMUNITY AND THE CRIMINAL CODE

The so-called inmate code is so strong in correctional institutions that an inmate may jeopardize his comfort and safety if he violates it. Many inmates are upset when they realize that participation in the correctional community means providing "feedback"—telling what goes on outside the group to the large group. This may involve violations of the institutional rules by inmates. Yet, unless the activities which occur in the dormitory or at work away from the large group are related in the community group, the program can make little progress. "Feedback" by improving communication enables the large group to focus its attention and energies on all possible here-and-now community problems. Adequate "feedback" allows the staff and inmates to face and discuss what transpires in the community throughout the day. Thus, feedback in action facilitates the positive community culture.

However, as Anecdotal Report 5 confirms, it continues to be difficult to communicate the importance and acceptability of "feedback" to newly arrived inmates. These new inmates, conditioned by the inmate code, regard the naming of an inmate and the describing of the wrong that he has done not as helpful but as an act of denunciation.

ANECDOTAL REPORT 5: Fluctuation in Feedback

A Community in Which Feedback Has Deteriorated. — A dormitory with sixty residents had established a good community culture. Delinquent behavior was fed back into the large group. The members of the community used such information to try to help their fellows. Gradually, however, the culture began to deteriorate. The "feedback" brought into the community group became less significant and rarely threatening. Trivia, like a member having an extra pair of socks in his locker, were fed back; however, nothing was said in the group about inmates who were known to the staff to be sniffing lighter fluid and paint thinner. So, the staff decided to bring such concerns into the group.

The responses of the inmates were typical of the criminal code. One of them asked, "What could we have done to stop the sniffing? If I had said anything to those sniffing, it would have started a fight." Another said, "The staff should have been more alert and controlled the situation." At this, a staff member asked the question, "What does the community plan to do to help these people?" Little anxiety was noted. The staff member then asked for the names of those who were sniffing. This was met with complete silence. At this point, some inmates offered the explanation that they could only go "so far." The group began to talk about the inmate culture, referring to it as "the code."

The staff's response was to ask what had caused the change in the community. The inmates had not been nearly so concerned about the "code" a few months back. One staff member asked, "Could this have happened because so many residents from this dormitory had been paroled? Were the new members the ones who were reinforcing the delinquent code?" Another staff member then asked, "Why can you only 'go so far,' and why can't you feed back the necessary information to help these people?" This aroused responses from the newer members of the community. They talked about the dangers of being labeled "finks." There were even comments about someone being hit over the head with a piece of iron pipe.

Finally, some of the more mature members of the community began to question all this. They said that they had fed back important information a few months ago and nobody was "piped" or labeled a "fink." Then its more delinquent members tried to frighten the group by talking about the possibility of someone being "shanked," or knifed. At this, the more mature members began to challenge this kind of thinking as unrealistic. The majority of the group were willing to restore genuine feedback.

The Inmates Are Confronted with Their Derelictions. — The remainder of this large-group meeting and most of the next was given over by the inmates to expressions of hostility toward the supervisor. Gradually, this attitude receded as some of the hostility was directed toward those who had sniffed the volatile solutions. It was repeatedly pointed out by the group members that if these persons really cared about the rest of the community, they would admit that they had been "sniffing" and take the rest "off the hook." For the moment, the social pressure in the dormitory was being focused on the few who had sniffed. Then, in a pique, one inmate commented that if the staff were more alert they would know who was doing the sniffing. Another said that by looking around the room you could almost tell the guilty parties from their faces. A staff member then explained that it was not nearly so important to determine who had been sniffing at this time as it was for the community to be concerned enough about the problem to help the ones who had been sniffing.

At the next meeting, one man admitted that he had been involved in the delinquent behavior. Then another inmate admitted his involvement. The supervisor noted that these confessions appeared to be more like "sacrificial offerings to the staff" than the acceptance by the community of responsibility and feedback restoration in order to help the guilty ones. It was pointed out that the two men who confessed had little to lose as they had only been in the program a short time. On the other hand, there were several members who had been in the community several months whose release would undoubtedly be affected if they were to make such confessions. Gradually, over the next two weeks, as the staff insisted that sniffing was a topic that must be discussed, others admitted their involvement.

Handling the Holdout. — Toward the end of the third week, the group indicated that only one inmate had not yet stated his involvement to the group. The men agreed resentfully that it would do no good to discuss his case as the man was not even attending the meeting; in fact, he was asleep in the dormitory. Thus, staff learned who the man was because only one man was asleep in the dormitory! The supervisor then asked what the group wanted to do. They agreed to go and have a group meeting by his bed. This was a painful learning experience for the man. Thus, the community resolved a crisis by moving away from the inmate code and toward feedback in the large group.

When the inmate code reappears, staff members must be patient and helpful in their conduct, and continue to express confidence that ultimately open communication will return to the community. For example, when a group was discussing the violation of a rule which occurred the previous night, an inmate said, "I can't mention any names, but . . .". This is an opportunity for a staff member to ask, "Why can't you mention any names?" Initially, if the group is an extremely delinquent one and functioning on a low maturity level, they will become disgusted with the staff member. They may make statements referring to his naïvete or point out the serious trouble that may occur if names are mentioned.

As time goes on, the staff can help the inmates to recognize the difference between "snitching" or telling on someone to put oneself in a good light, and feedback which means bringing the person and his behavior out in the open in order to help him. At first, inmates are usually not able to mention the names of persons guilty of delinquent behavior. They do, however, seem able to work with these individuals in a confidential way without involving staff so that they may be able to indicate to them the need for more control of the delinquent behavior. Later on, the members may begin to understand that sometimes a person has to be hurt in order to be helped. In a good community group, the men become convinced that bringing the name of a person and his behavior out into the open is essential to frank discussion and resolution of problems. As feedback becomes more generally accepted in the community, it overcomes the delinquent code.

The prerequisite, then, for open communication is that, first, all staff members and inmates become concerned about each other's welfare; and, second, that the interpersonal relationships within the community are so well developed that they can support behavior that violates the delinquent code. The more concern a member of the community feels for another, the better able he is to bring out information concerning this other member's delinquent behavior. And with this development it becomes more difficult for the one having his behavior fed back into the group to become angry and bitter with the others.

As illustrated in Anecdotal Report 5, the leaders of the correctional community cannot rest upon their oars and feel satisfied that they have solved the problem of getting feedback in the group. Instead, they must realize that because of changes in group membership, this cannot be a static, unchanging situation. Within a community, there are cycles of progression and regression toward and away from the most desirable community feeling and responsibility. The staff must be alert at all times. When they begin to feel that members of the community are becoming less interested in each other, they can also assume that the feedback responsibility is beginning to deteriorate. This is exemplified by comments like: "I am just interested in doing my own time"; "I have enough troubles of my own without worrying about anyone else"; "How can I help a person who doesn't want my help anyway?" Statements of this type are usually precipitated by some delinquent behavior in the community which has come to the staff's attention outside of the large group. These circumstances indicate that the community has begun to slide backwards. At this point, the efforts of the staff should not be directed so much toward resolving any particular delinquent situation, but should focus on bringing the community back to their aims and purposes. In many cases, this means not focusing on individual delinquent behavior but on the fact that the community did not assume its responsibilities and allowed the behavior to occur.

In summarizing this important basic problem in the correctional community, we must recognize that feedback is an important tool. It is the barometer of how well the community is progressing or regressing in mutual helpfulness. Lastly, feedback is breaking down the delinquent culture and directing the energies of the group toward treatment and rehabilitation.

THE AUTHORITY OF COMPETENCE

When the goals of the correctional community are being realized, the inmates begin to look upon the staff as persons whose authority they respect because of their competence to be helpful to them. Their faith is like that of a patient in a physician who, because the patient perceives him as competent in his professional role, accepts him as an authority. This is the beginning of mutual trust and respect.

To achieve this authority of competency in the eyes of the inmates, the staff does not forego its responsibility for setting and maintaining rules. In fact, this limit-setting may be regarded as helpful and not harmful when coming from one who has The Authority of Competence. When a doctor, accepted as an authority, limits a patient's activities by ordering him to bed, the patient may not like the order, but he does not feel resentful toward the doctor. He recognizes that the order is for his own well-being.

What does a staff member do in the large group or elsewhere in the correctional community to establish himself in the minds of the inmates as a competent authority figure? He must meet three requirements:

First, in the large group he must function as an objective adult rather than a protecting or moralistic parent substitute. Staff participation in the community group should be as objective as possible and leave the inmates to indulge in moral judgment about social behavior if they choose. The staff does not need to point out to the inmates what is right or wrong. Many observations have shown that delinquents and criminals are not defective in knowledge of the differences between good and bad. Deciding whether some thought or action is right or wrong usually poses no difficulties for inmates. They do, in fact, know high ethical standards and set them for others, notably members of institutional staffs. Their problems in society resulted from not avoiding what they knew to be wrong.

The role of the staff as authority figures helps inmates to understand the meaning and consequences of their delinquent behavior. This is done in as nonthreatening and nonmoralizing a manner as possible. Inmate opinions and attitudes should be formed as a result of their own changing view of reality and not as a result of the demands or persuasion of authority figures. When inmates are not forced to defend themselves against condemnation from authorities, they are better able to believe in their own good judgment.

Second, a staff member must be able to make the inmates feel that when he sets limits he does so to help them and not to reinforce his own status or to exercise authority. If an orderly society is to exist, there must be limits of behavior. This can be stated to the group. But in imposing limits in the correctional community, the staff member must also convince the inmates by his actions that these limits are reasonable and logical. They are for the benefit of the individuals as well as for the group. Obedience to restrictions will come about more willingly after the inmates trust the competence of the staff.

A third factor which helps inmates accept the authority of a staff member comes from the latter's ability to give the inmates the feeling that he regards them as potentially wholesome persons. In doing so, the member must be able to convince the inmates that it is possible to separate each man from his delinquent behavior. Though the staff member disapproves of the inmate's delinquent *behavior*, he does not reject the *person*. In this he is like the doctor who may not like the fact that the patient contacted venereal disease, but helps him without criticizing or rejecting him as a person. This is a difficult task for many members of the staff because of strong prejudices, and because physical illness is so much more acceptable than delinquent behavior.

The staff member progresses toward the Authority of Competence to the extent that he succeeds in meeting these requirements in his daily relations with the inmates in the large group and elsewhere. The three requirements are: to be objective and not moralistic in his judgments of inmates; to present rules in such a way that an inmate can see values in them for himself; and to believe in the potential of inmates to make satisfactory adjustments in the "free world."

INMATE GROWTH IN RESPONSIBILITY

Many inmates in correctional institutions seem to be unwilling or unable to assume responsibility. Traditionally, prison staffs have encouraged this failing by giving inmates practically no responsibility for handling their own affairs in prison. As time passes, inmates become more dependent, less responsible, and less self-reliant. Upon parole release, many are less competent in taking care of their own affairs than before the commitment.

When returned as parole violators, these men may welcome their dependent status in the institution. They become increasingly poor risks for ultimate adjustment in the outside community.

If failure among parolees is due in part to a dependency conflict, it seems appropriate to train inmates to assume responsibilities through practical experiences during their institutional stay. Objections may be offered to this suggestion by staff members who fear difficulties in the operation of the prisons. Such fear leads to the conviction that inmates must be forced to work and not given real responsibility—not even for keeping their dormitories clean. It seems easier and less threatening to use close supervision and the threat of punishment to get dormitories clean.

The effectiveness of a correctional community program depends upon the inmates assuming responsibility. In a sense, this is an antidote to the many destructive "institutionalizing" features of prison. Within reasonable limits, the staff of a correctional community must find ways and means of fostering inmate responsibility. By assuming responsibility, inmates assume more self-respect, independence, and interdependence.

However, the staff of the correctional community must maintain their basic responsibility for the conduct of the institution and their public obligations for proper management. The following Anecdotal Report illustrates these issues.

ANECDOTAL REPORT 6: Responsibility in Towel Distribution

Initial Experiences after Giving Inmates Responsibility. — In a 60-man dormitory, the inmates brought their soiled towels to a central location where, after being counted, clean ones were issued. This had been a carefully monitored routine procedure. The correctional community staff in this dormitory decided to increase the prisoners' responsibility beginning with a different procedure in distributing towels. One morning, it was explained in the large group that towels would be given out on Monday, Wednesday, and Friday of each week, by simply being placed on a conveniently located table, one towel for each inmate.

First Returns from the Plan. — The program started on the following day when 60 towels were placed on the designated table. The inmates scrambled for them. Some took more than one. Staff made no move to control the situation. The individuals who did not get towels were angry and attempted to manipulate the staff to get towels. Staff refused, explaining that 60 towels had been placed on the table, enough for all. The responsibility for towel distribution belonged with the inmates. Some inmates threatened that "something drastic" might result if staff didn't handle the problem.

When their demands were not met, some inmates showered and came to the staff nude, dripping wet, and explained that they had no towels. The staff explained that they understood this situation, but did not supply towels. The inmates were bitter and again threatened that some inmate might be beaten up or "piped" that evening if the staff did not act. The threats were ignored. Thus frustrated, the wet inmates asked the staff what they should do and how they could dry off. Staff said they would have to work the problem out for themselves. The inmates then returned to the shower and used their underwear for towels.

The next morning in the community-group meeting, the inmates let loose a barrage of hostility. They questioned whether the staff was really interested in helping them. They complained that the State of California was too cheap to provide enough towels. They made wild comments and menacing gestures in an effort to manipulate staff. When it became apparent to them that the staff would not be stampeded or manipulated, the atmosphere changed. One inmate suggested a solution. Those without towels could report to the gym and state that they were going to work out. The coach would then provide them with towels. Instead of working out, the inmates could return to the dormitory with these towels. The supervisor asked, "Isn't this a delinquent solution to the problem? Is it not in fact somewhat like the kind of behavior which had gotten you into the institution in the first place?" At this the inmate blushed, others laughed.

More Maturity is Evidenced. — Finally, one inmate pointed out that the group could assume the responsibility for seeing that everyone got a towel. But the group was not yet ready to accept this answer to their situation. This problem continued to be talked about in groups for six weeks. Some staff members became bored and wanted to change the subject. Actually, they were becoming more anxious and frustrated, and wanted to talk about more comfortable subjects. The supervisor maintained that this subject should be talked about until the community could handle this responsibility. By insisting that the inmates assume responsibility for proper distribution of the sixty towels, the staff was able to assist the inmates of accepting the responsibility of seeing to it that each inmate took only one towel, and that there was a towel for each. In this manner the inmates, rather than the staff, were responsible.

Lessons from the Report. — This may seem to be a trivial responsibility. Actually, it was important as the beginning of growth in responsibility. The incident offers several lessons: The inmates may resist accepting responsibility for community management, by criticizing and blaming everyone but themselves, making threats of imminent incidents or violence to intimidate the staff, or resorting to childish antics like the wet and naked inmates who came to the supervisor.

If the staff is to be useful in the correctional-community program, they must learn to handle their own anxieties in the community group. They must also not be concerned over the amount of time taken by these issues. The vital role of the post-session becomes apparent at these times of crisis in providing significant training.

When an unresolved and disturbing problem is before the group for a long period, the community-group sessions may become threatening to the staff of the housing unit and top administrators in the institution. Staff must have confidence in the belief that the correctional-community approach brings about "better management." But operations will not be smooth and without tension forevermore. Staff must remain steadfast in allowing the community to make mistakes and to learn from these mistakes. In fact, Bateson (2), Rapoport (24, pp. 166–167), and Wilmer (37, p. 32) agree that it is doubtful that anything therapeutically significant can occur unless the community is constantly undergoing and resolving crisis situations like these.

Anecdotal Report 7 illustrates the painful and arduous efforts of a community of inmates to control pilfering in its midst.

ANECDOTAL REPORT 7: The Unlocked Lockers

A Self-Centered Group. – A new supervisor was assigned to a 6o-man dormitory community. This community group was behaving selfishly, with little concern for each other. Each individual was interested in "doing his own time and getting out." For two months the staff tried to develop a community atmosphere of mutual concern in interpersonal relations.

A Drastic Experiment. – The staff finally decided upon a drastic experiment. They ordered the inmates to turn in the locks from their lockers. The request was based on the expectation that if the dormitory members became anxious about the valuables in their lockers, they might work together as a community with real concern for each other's property. When the plan was announced, in the large group, the inmates reacted strongly against it. They said that men from the other dormitories might come and steal their possessions. "How could we handle this problem if the stealing is by outsiders?" To this objection, the supervisor created a rule: there would be no visiting by inmates from other dormitories. Still the inmates saw a loophole: while they were away at meal times, outsiders might come and rob them. The supervisor stated that this was a problem they would have to solve for themselves. The inmates accepted this responsibility and decided to vary their meal times so that someone would be present while the others were in the mess hall.

Fluctuating Progress toward Responsibility. – Gradually, by assuming responsibility for each other's property, they began to show more concern for each other's behavior. Still, there remained a feeling in the dormitory that at any time someone still might be tempted to take something from another's locker.

Approximately three weeks before Christmas, the group members said that they had been able to operate effectively without their locks and had made progress in "community living." After this declaration, they said that having demonstrated their capacity to accept responsibility, they no longer needed to live without their locks and requested that they be returned. The supervisor suspected that the real desire for the locks was the result of their fears that the forthcoming arrival of Christmas gifts would break down the social control. The supervisor said he appreciated their feelings but felt that the locks should not be returned. This statement aroused protests and threats of retaliation if anything were taken from the lockers.

Anxiety over the Loss of Christmas Gifts. – During Christmas week, the inmates lost faith. Most members took their Christmas foods to other dormitories where locks were on the lockers. This discouraged the staff because the inmates circumvented the problem. However, it turned out that their plan did not work out as they had hoped; some of their Christmas candies and cakes were eaten by their "friends."

A Crisis Occurs. – Then one day an inmate put a lock back on his locker, in violation of a rule. A disciplinary report was written. Some members of the group had been stealing from his locker, so he purchased a lock from the canteen. The community group now discussed that the inmate had used the lock to protect his possessions. They concluded that they all ought to be permitted to do the same. The supervisor listened, then insisted that this was a community problem. The inmates reminded the staff that they had stated that if inmates demonstrated inability to handle a problem, staff would take over. The supervisor replied that the dormitory community was mature enough to handle the problem themselves. At this, the group almost unanimously commanded the inmate to remove the lock from his locker. He refused. The others said that if he removed the lock he would not lose his possessions because now they would assume the responsibility. Some inmates, whose beds were near his, volunteered to provide a special watch for a few weeks to make good this assurance. Because of the reassurance from the group, the inmate complied with the group request.

Comments. – The lock problem had remained a community topic for two and one-half months. Before the removal of the locks, if an inmate lost anything from his locker, he blamed himself for not locking his locker, or he threatened to "get even" with someone. After the community agreed to be responsible for stealing, pilfering ceased almost entirely. This was a group victory over the inmate code.

AREAS IN WHICH RESPONSIBILITY
WAS ASSIGNED TO INMATES

The following examples of inmates assuming responsible roles in daily dormitory life are cited as evidence of the potential for social maturity of prisoners in a correctional therapeutic community.

Control of Television. — Television is a common recreational experience for all inmates in the dormitory. It is a reasonable area in which the community group can face their social responsibility for the hours permitted for television; for the channels selected; and for a definition of acceptable behavior during the watching time. The control of television offers an excellent opportunity to handle a "here and now" problem of group-living in an area of concern to everyone in the community.

Arrangements Regarding the Use of Radios. — In most large institutions three stations are selected by the staff and transmitted to the housing unit. Inmates who usually have earphones can select a program. In a 60-bed housing unit, the inmates were permitted to obtain small radios of their own. To provide earphones for each set was not practical. Two problems concerning the use of radios that the inmates had to resolve were: the hours when they could be turned on, and the loudness of the volume.

Arising in the Morning and Retiring at Night. — Within limits, responsibility for arising and retiring can be assumed by the inmates. At first, many inmates are not able to cope with either of these responsibilities. In one dormitory an inmate simply refused to get up in the morning, so the staff decided to let him sleep as long as he wished even though they were afraid that the entire dormitory might decide to sleep in. For a time, his behavior became a dormitory joke. As the other group members did not join his "one-man strike" or approve his behavior, he became worried. In the large group, his peers told him that his self-defeating behavior was related to the problems which caused him to be sent to prison. The inmates, not the staff, told him that unless he would "wise up and grow up," he would probably fail on parole. After this group meeting, he got up on time. The staff might have forced him to get up through disciplinary methods, but the impact of the inmates as a group was of greater learning value and more effective from a practical point of view. It not only affected the delinquent inmate but also the strength and self-respect of the group itself.

Other examples. — Group responsibility for control of feeding; inmate responsibility in the institutional classification program; and staff responsibility for selection and maximum use of vocational, academic, recreational, and religious programs are other examples of areas permitting growth in responsibility in the correctional community.

CONFLICT BETWEEN STAFF AND INMATES

When the large group reaches an impasse, the situation demands careful reasoning to understand its cause. How did the inmates and the staff arrive at the impasse? The resolution of an impasse gives the staff experience and competence in coping more effectively with a similar problem in the future. The situation described in Anecdotal Report 8 illustrates how the lack of harmony between the staff and the inmates in the large group resulted in an impasse; the inmates believed the staff was punitive and uncompromising, and the staff felt the inmates were immature and uncompromising.

ANECDOTAL REPORT 8: Conflict over Control of Contraband

Whose Responsibility Is the Control of Contraband? — The staff in attempting to make inroads on the delinquent culture, reported in the large-group meeting that many members of the community had contraband in their possessions. The inmates showed no concern. They indicated that this was a staff problem.

The staff felt that the more mature inmates were not enough concerned to solve the problem. The staff was dissatisfied because the community group would not accept this responsibility. The staff felt a need to "hurt them" for the inmates' indifferent response to what they thought should be a community responsibility. Consequently, the staff notified the community that there would be no more TV-viewing until they began to handle this problem. The staff, in doing this, was wrong, but this merely illustrates that the staff is human and can err, and must show maturity and ability to correct their mistakes so that inmates can form healthy identifications. The conflict caused a division of the community into two factions—residents and staff, both insisting that they were right, and resulted in a "stand-off." The residents saw staff inflicting "mass punishment," and the staff saw the residents as "resistant."

The Staff Studies the "Stand-off" Situation. — In the post-group session, the staff discussed its need to "punish" the inmates. The supervisor pointed out that if certain privileges were going to be withdrawn when the community was functioning inadequately, this should have been spelled out clearly to the community group before any action was taken.

The following criteria could be used to inform the inmates what is meant by a "responsible community":

Delinquent behavior is openly discussed in the community meetings;

Each member is concerned about the behavior of every other member;

The members of the group genuinely try to help one another understand and handle the problems they relate to the group;

The group demonstrates responsibility not only for each other, but also for the community as a whole.

STAFF ADMISSION OF ERROR
MAY REPRESENT STRENGTH

To break an impasse often requires that the staff admit where they have made a mistake. Usually this prompts inmates to look more objectively at their own behavior and to recognize how they contributed to the "stand-off." Inexperienced staff members may fear that admitting a mistake will weaken their staff authority and control. When the staff decides to admit a mistake, this is evidence of error, not of weakness, and reveals a strength. The result has usually been increasing respect. This may be completely opposite to what a new staff member anticipates. However, staff, by learning from their mistakes, must not continue to make the same error.

ANECDOTAL REPORT 9: Staff Must also Accept Responsibility

An Appointment Is Not Kept. — An inmate in the community requested an interview with the unit supervisor. The supervisor replied that he was busy at the moment, but would see him in his office after lunch the following day. Due to an emergency meeting with the superintendent, the staff member was unable to keep the appointment with the inmate. In fact, he forgot it. The following morning the staff member came to the large group. After much time spent talking about the importance of each man's responsibilities, the forgotten prisoner pointedly said that it was equally important for staff to assume their responsibilities. To this the staff members agreed. Then he asked the erring staff member if it was not his responsibility to keep his appointments "even with an inmate." The staff member then recalled the forgotten appointment.

The Staff Member Admits His Error. — At first, the staff member's impulse was to justify his negligence by explaining that the superintendent had called him in to an emergency meeting. Instead of doing this the staff member agreed that it had been his responsibility to meet the resident yesterday afternoon or to tell him of the impossibility of meeting him and reschedule the appointment and that he had fallen down in his responsibilities, adding that he had no valid excuse. The defense of the staff member came first from the inmate himself and then from the community. They understood that as supervisor of the unit, he had many responsibilities which might make it necessary for him to break an appointment. The outcome of the episode was that the staff member's stature grew.

THE LOCATION OF DISCIPLINARY HEARINGS

As the culture of the community group matures, staff members may wish to consider holding some of the disciplinary hearings in the community group. This is not recommended unless the staff is certain that the community is functioning well and using good judgment. When the group acts immaturely, the inmates feel they must support each other's delinquency according to the "inmate code." They must unite together in order to protect themselves against hostile and punitive authorities. Therefore, when the staff is inexperienced or the community group is immature, disciplinary-committee meetings should be held in the traditional manner; that is, by a staff committee seeing only the affected inmate involved. The staff must then relate the results to the group.

If, however, the staff is experienced and skilled, and if time is available for the disciplinary hearing to be held in the large meeting, this method has often proved to be valuable for the development of the correctional community. When the disciplinary hearings are held in the group meeting, they are better understood by everyone. The assistance of the inmates may be helpful. This is not to say that the staff should turn over disciplinary responsibilities to the inmates, but rather that staff should work with inmates in order to cope with self-defeating, delinquent behavior. Anecdotal Report 10 illustrates the use of the community in resolving a disciplinary matter.

Anecdotal Report 10: A Disciplinary Hearing in the Community

Glue-Sniffing. — In a mature dormitory community, two new inmate members were cited in disciplinary reports for misbehavior at 2 o'clock in the morning: one for not being in his bed; the other for sniffing glue. The disciplinary hearings for these men were held in the community group. Present were the 60 inmates, the correctional counselor, the correctional officer, and the hearing officer. After the two disciplinary reports were read, the hearing officer asked the inmates if the facts were accurate. The offender who had been away from his bed after "lights out" stated that they were true in his case. The other inmate who had received a disciplinary report for sniffing glue denied the facts. The only evidence that he might have been sniffing glue was a medical report of a "strange odor on his breath." The inmate claimed that except for the strange odor on his breath, he had passed all "sobriety" tests. In answer to a question from the hearing officer the inmate replied that he had been in the group only one month.

The Group Assists in the Hearing. — The hearing officer stated that he was not interested in holding a formal disciplinary session but instead wanted to help the men solve their problems. He asked

the inmates in the community if they would help the defensive and
uncooperative member. After a brief silence, one inmate stated that
most of the staff and inmates knew that he had sniffed glue. What
they wanted to know was why he did, and what he himself could
do about this harmful behavior. This comment, at variance with the
delinquent code, upset the inmate, and he continued to claim he
was innocent. Another inmate, ignoring the denial, stated that he
understood the wife of the man who had been sniffing glue was
seeking a divorce, and that this might be related to his glue-sniffing
episode. The accused resident seemed to collapse as he denied that
pressure from his marital problem was the reason for his sniffing
glue. He now admitted that he had sniffed glue but could not explain why. The hearing officer then asked the other offender (who
had not been in bed) how long he had been in the dormitory. His
answer was, "one month." The hearing officer then asked this resident if he had been sniffing glue. He admitted he had, but had not
been caught.

The Efforts at Treatment Are Led by the Inmates. — When these
two men recognized that the staff and the community were interested in helping them rather than "trapping" or "hurting" them,
the discussion changed dramatically. Both inmates said they felt
"rejected" in the dormitory; no one had in any way welcomed them.
One said he was lonesome and attempted to escape from this discomfort by sniffing. The other vainly sought acceptance in the group
by his delinquent behavior. The feeling of the community group
was that it would take some time for these two men to adapt to the
community's expectations. As a result of these hearings, the two
men were required to develop a plan for a more adequate reception
of newly received residents so others would not have to learn by
trial and error. They asked three others to help prepare an orientation plan which would explain the operation and purpose of the
correctional therapeutic community.

When the final disciplinary disposition is discussed with the
community group they should be aware of the broader considerations of institutional management. For example, in a large
institution it is sometimes necessary to demonstrate that a certain behavior is not acceptable. Therefore, the final disposition
may not only help the affected inmate but also communicate to
others the limits of acceptable behavior. Inmate community

groups can accept the fact that sometimes punishment is necessary for purposes of communicating to others standards of behavior that must be maintained for management control needs.
For example:

ANECDOTAL REPORT 11: Disciplinary Help from the Peer Group

An inmate had received a disciplinary report for failing to obey an
order. When leaving the mess hall, he had thrown a metal container in the garbage bucket and when he was requested to remove
it and place it in the appropriate container, he refused.

The disciplinary report was read in the large group. The community group questioned the inmate why he had conducted himself
in the manner mentioned. From the discussion which followed, it
became apparent that he felt it was beneath him to place his hands
in the garbage to remove the metal container. The group was able
to recall other situations which had not been brought to the attention of the staff in which he had behaved similarly. They asked
him if he was aware that some other inmate would have to assume
his responsibility by picking the container out of the garbage.

This situation was painful and uncomfortable for the inmate who
had to look at his behavior through the eyes of others who saw him
"too good to do the common man's work." Nevertheless, there was
a feeling of understanding for him.

The staff told the community group that since they were one
60-man community in an institution with eighteen other such communities, the disciplinary action would not only be in terms of helping the inmate but to communicate to the other inmate groups that
this kind of behavior would not be tolerated.

After some discussion, the group felt that for one day of meals
(breakfast, lunch, and dinner) the violating inmate would have to
go to the mess hall and assume the duties of taking care of the
garbage bucket and removing the foreign objects. This would communicate to all inmates that the criticized behavior was not acceptable. The inmate was not hostile over this disposition although he
stated that he did not like it. He seemed to sense that the group
was doing this in his interest and not to hurt him.

Even the best community becomes anxious when disciplinary
action is discussed. Often their recommendation for disposition
is unrealistic because of the overidentification for the involved

inmate, and the staff, in discussion with the group, must arrive at an equitable disposition. In community groups where this situation becomes too threatening, the staff should withdraw to make the final decision and take it back to the community group with their reasoning. This is an area which needs more exploration and research to determine the best method, but it is believed that the open and community-involved approach has more to offer in terms of a living-learning experience. Nevertheless, it should be recognized that this approach demands an advanced community group and skilled staff.

THE NATURE AND FUNCTIONS
OF THE SMALL GROUP

In defining the efforts of youth workers in an urban neighborhood to cope with delinquent adolescents, Spergel (30, p. 64) has listed three areas on which the application of correctional efforts may be focused: community organization, group work, and casework. Translated for the institutional correctional worker, these three areas are rather like those in the institutional correctional community. This parallel may be better appreciated by reference to the following statement by Maxwell Jones, (19, p. 87): "The correctional counselor may wish to continue individual treatment with some of his caseload. This is in no way incompatible with the small group and community meetings."

In a forestry camp for eighty men where the community is rather isolated and all activities of group-living are readily observed it is simple to think of the correctional institution as a community. But in a large prison for a thousand or more inmates, it is more difficult to think of this institution in community terms. Its subdivisions or "neighborhoods" consist of housing units for one hundred men or more or of smaller dormitory units.

In trying to achieve a wholesome law-abiding life in a society or community, constructive forces must play upon all the citizens. These must originate first in the over-all total community, second, in the neighborhood, and third, within the person himself, through effective individual casework. The helpful influences and forces in the correctional community are roughly like those originating in the large and small groups and in the individual. It may not be possible to point out exactly what their impact may be upon individuals or groups, or when improvement occurs—to say exactly how an individual or a group may have been helped.

Spergel (30) asks: "What are the larger societal pressures that may account for delinquent orientation?" The members of the institutional staff who set up the correctional community may wisely also ask themselves that question. Then they might seek methods for recognizing and combating the antisocial pressures in the total institutional environment. In the large or community group, staff will try to develop forces to counteract the atmosphere or conditions conducive to antisocial behavior in the institution arising in the delinquent culture, discussed in chapter 1.

The nature of the total positive forces for resocialization in the community group, has been stated by Jones (19, pp. 87–88): "The content of the discussion was not of prime importance. It was more the feeling that there was a body of interested people participating in something with which each individual could feel identified." The attitudes and the behavior of the staff were included in this force of "interested people" which strongly and helpfully affected the community atmosphere. The feelings of everyone in the community group were vital parts of this force for resocialization. In the correctional institution, the existence of these wholesome feelings is greatly dependent upon staff attitudes and feelings. The evidence of their acceptance of the inmates as fellow human beings and the avoidance of critical judgments, attitudes, or statements about them as persons, bring forth feelings of mutual tolerance and the relaxation of hostilities, suspicions, or worries in the inmates. This mutual acceptance creates a high level of helpfulness.

Group workers are faced with a similarly difficult problem in the advancement of more acceptable attitudes toward good citizenship in the outside community. The specific methods of the correctional community in the institution may differ from those which can be used with delinquents in a society on the outside. The eventual ideal of the institutional correctional community is the development of an over-all atmosphere conducive to preparing inmates to live within the law when they resume their places in society. Rapoport has epitomized this ideal in the title of his book, *The Community as Doctor* (24). Is this task less formidable in the simpler life situation in the institution than in the outside community?

FORERUNNERS OF THE SMALL GROUP

Forerunners of attempts to treat inmates in groups preceded by many years the introduction of the correctional community in the California correctional system. According to Schmidt (26) group treatment first began in 1933 as psychotherapy with small groups at San Quentin. When the Reception-Guidance Centers were established, academic teachers with training in educational counseling began to conduct group-counseling in somewhat larger numbers, sometimes as many as twenty-five. Usually they spent about three hours daily in group-counseling in the Reception Guidance Centers, during a period of four weeks. An estimate made about 1950 indicated that more than 90 percent of the total population of the California prisons had had this introductory experience in group-counseling.

A broader use of group counseling (10) was begun in 1954 as part of the institutional-treatment program. This group-counseling served as staff preparation for the correctional community because all employees were eligible to apply for training and later to participate in the program. By its influence upon a thousand or more staff members of all job classifications, many of whom had joined the treatment program as active participants for the first time, group-counseling undoubtedly played a major role in the later acceptance of the correctional community.

Observations of how large and small groups are conducted in the correctional community indicate that employees are applying the permissive methods with which they had become familiar in group-counseling. The groups are not guided by staff desires or moralistic preachings; their activities are self-initiated and the discussion has an immediate and serious relevance to the lives of the inmates.

A volume could be written about the many constructive developments, including group-counseling, that preceded the beginning and advancement of the correctional community. In what follows, five major factors have been selected for brief summary among many that might be mentioned. Without them there would probably have been less readiness for an adequate try-out of the correctional community in the California prisons.

The first factor was the professionalization of adult correctional work. After the Department of Corrections of California was established in 1944, under the leadership of Richard A. McGee, a career penologist, one of the first important developments was the improvement of the standards of employment and job stability. This was done in 1945 by including the Department of Corrections into the State Civil Service system. Since then, the merit system of employment and promotion has been an important element in the recruitment of personnel for the correctional institutions.

A second factor during the same period was the establishment of the Reception-Guidance Centers which resulted in the recruitment of many clinicians. Associated with these advances in clinical diagnosis was the development of confidentiality in the departmental records denying inmates access to inmate files, and making them available to authorized personnel only. More extensive case materials from welfare, judicial, and law-enforcement agencies were sent thereafter to the Department of Corrections. The prisons were recognized as acceptable and responsible in the use of the facilities of local social-service exchanges.

Third, a simultaneous increase in the treatment staffs in the institutions improved the likelihood of carrying out recommendations from the diagnostic studies of newly received inmates. Included among these additional employees were medical, educational, psychiatric, psychological, recreational, religious, and social-service personnel. Another feature of the transition toward treatment in the prisons was the recruitment of skilled supervisors and foremen for industrial and maintenance work for inmates.

Fourth, a *comprehensive* program of in-service training was introduced. Since 1945, all employees in the prisons and in the parole divisions have participated in staff-training programs. Attendance at many hours of in-service training each year has been and now is a recognized part of their work, for which they are compensated. This instruction has paved the way for employee interest in training programs about the correctional community.

Finally, a division of research was created in 1957. Through its encouragement of experimentation in the program, the research staff has been a notable force in the development of the correctional community.

These five examples of earlier contributions to the program brought the California correctional system to the necessary professional level for the acceptance of the treatment development called "the correctional community."

THE SMALL GROUP

The optimal size of the small group seems to be about ten or twelve inmates. One employee may conduct the group alone or in coleadership with others on the staff. The small group may meet once or twice a week or even daily, and for at least an hour. Sessions may be held in shops, offices, dormitory corridors, classrooms, and even outdoors. Groups are usually open and continuous. As one member leaves, another is permitted to join. Rarely used in the correctional community is the closed group to which, once begun, new inmates are not added. Wilmer (37, p. 38) believes that an ever-changing population is "beneficial to the community," because it thereby "faces new challenges by getting new 'siblings' and losing others."

The small group is closely related to the large or community group. The leaders and inmates of the small groups meet in the

large group; besides, if possible, others on the staff, such as vocational instructors or maintenance foremen, are asked to attend regularly.

Discussions may start in either group and be continued in
the other. The inmates are made aware that what is discussed
anywhere can be brought up again either by them or by staff
members in the small or large groups. There is no emphasis
upon strict confidentiality either in the large or small group.
According to some exponents of the correctional community, the
inmates have no secrets from each other, except what they withhold completely from the community. Whatever is divulged
anywhere in the correctional community, in the individual conference or in the small group, may become the common knowledge of the larger institutional community. Chamlee (7, p. 8)
has stated this point of view: "Virtually no information is seen
as confidential except that case-file material which is restricted
by virtue of law or Departmental policy." "No communications
are seen as privileged. More to the point is 'how or when' the
information or 'feed-back' is used. The emphasis should be on
timing and appropriateness rather than on content. One-to-one
relationships, small groups, family groups, 'spontaneous' groups
are seen as detrimental to the effectiveness of the milieu, if
information revealed in them does not get back to the total
community."

If the inmates are to be helped to adjust to their emotional
problems, if the community is to be "the doctor," the members
of the community must know about these intimate matters.
Presumably, if the members of the group were unaware of what
was troubling an inmate, they could not help him. The inmates
would continue to be harassed by attitudes and feelings, many
of which may have played serious parts in their crimes and con-
victions. The operation of a correctional community on this
level requires a fully qualified and trained staff and a group of
inmates who will work together for many months. Not all groups
function at this level nor even do the more experienced groups
usually maintain consistently this level of treatment sophisti-
cation.

COMPARISON OF THE SMALL GROUP WITH OTHER OPERATIONS

Within the therapeutic community, the small group is considered by Jones (19), Wilmer (37) and other leaders in community therapy to be an important part of the total treatment program. Its functions support the large or community group. If we think of the large group as a community, then we may consider the small group as having some of the characteristics of a family. Weldon H. Smith (29, p. 3) in describing the correctional community in an institution for inmates who had been addicted to the use of narcotics, made this point as he defined the nature and status of the small group: "A small group was considered as a primary treatment vehicle for the program. It was here in the smaller, family concept that the addict was encouraged by his peers to make his beginnings in the program." According to Smith the small group offers a greater sense of security when the inmates discuss their most personal problems for the first time in a group.

Heim (17, p. 29), who conducted an interesting study of inmate perceptions of the correctional community, confirmed this point of view: The men he studied regarded the small groups as "tightly knit families." He also reported that the small group was perceived "as close, friendly, warm, less defensive, more gentle, and more relaxed. The men mentioned feelings of togetherness, greater patience and tolerance, freer communication, greater comfort, and believed the small groups to be more effective treatment-wise." To the previous comments about "the more gentle and relaxed" smaller group, we should add Wilmer's point (37, p. 32) that anxiety should be present in the small group if treatment is to occur: "The aim of the therapeutic community is not peace but the use of tension through a continuing review of social positions, of behavior, of motivation."

Heim (17, p. 37) summarized another difference between small and large groups as perceived by the inmates as follows: "Finally, that the men seemed more themselves and less 'phony' in the small groups was puzzling. One subject thought it was because fewer staff were present, abating the need to put on a front. Yet it was well known that what transpired in the small groups was reported at meetings of the entire staff. Perhaps it is a matter of being able to be yourself because those closest to you have learned what you really are and the pretense is thus felt to be necessary only with persons less well known." Seemingly, the small group develops its own morale. Inmates bring up personal matters which they are unwilling to talk about at first in the large group. In the small group, as others in the group venture to discuss subjects closest to their hearts, the more repressed or suspicious inmates gain courage by their examples to divulge their own problems. No one should ever be ridiculed, baited, or insulted because of the nature of the troubles he reveals. Very soon after its establishment, as the Heim quotations suggest, mutual sympathy and good will permeate the small group. In the long run, this atmosphere is transmitted to the large group, especially if the inmates accept the over-all leadership of the program with trust and comfort.

OTHER VIEWS ON THE SMALL GROUP

The cited favorable comments about the values of the small group are contradicted by the experiences of workers in other places. In contrast to the point of view of Weldon H. Smith (29) quoted earlier, some staff members have discussed the desirability of discontinuing the small groups, at least temporarily, if material discussed in it does not reach the large group.

Perhaps the more important lesson to be gained from this controversy is that the small and large groups must have closely integrated objectives. The large-group meeting is often a dynamic process, very demanding of inmates and staff. It requires honest self-examination, and a willingness not only to face unpleasant aspects of one's self, but to acknowledge and discuss these with others. It is easy to understand why inmates and staff have viewed the small group or individual sessions as "better" or "friendlier." In truth, through allowing them to become less anxiety-producing, they thereby become less capable of being effective. There seems to be an almost universal resistance to the large-group meeting by inmates and staff at first. The setting is threatening. It is not always easy to follow and understand the discussion. Often the outcome of discussions in the large-group meetings are not satisfying to either inmates or staff. Generally speaking, only staff members well-trained in group methods and with considerable experience in handling the community groups feel comfortable and are able to handle adequately the inmate problems in the large group.

The large-community group meeting must be considered the primary forum to solve immediate problems and meet crises of the institutional community; in this regard, the role of the small group is secondary. Any discussions by inmates of community problems in the small group must be diligently fed back to the large group either by the inmates or by the staff. If, in doing so, serious obstacles are encountered, it may be necessary to limit discussions of community problems to the large group. Thus, the staff must be aware of any tendency to give priority to the more "comfortable" setting of the small group. When the small group predominates, the large-group meeting, and also the total community atmosphere, will begin to deteriorate.

If the objectives of the correctional community are accepted by inmates and staff, then large groups, small groups, and individual casework can function together harmoniously and productively. If honest and open communication exists, and with it a willingness by those in the community group to be confronted by their inconsistencies, half-truths, rationalizations, and projections and to work through these confrontations, then these desirable events can occur in large or small groups or in individual settings. It must be repeated for emphasis that there is a danger for settings other than the large group to be used to avoid and deny rather than to accept the fundamental purposes of community treatment.

Those who favor the continued use of the small group consider it valuable for initial discussions of personal problems of the kind that inmates would shy away from bringing up in the large group. As inmates feel comfortable there, the small group becomes a place in which those present, according to this viewpoint, feel freer to disclose intimate matters. In view of the suspicion and resistance of inmates to the acceptance of the staff as worthy and thus trustworthy the small group is necessary and preparatory to the large group. It is also a place for continued discussion of topics arising in the large group. Small groups in this sense provide a setting where the less verbal, slower-thinking, and more withdrawn inmates can express themselves and resolve their concerns.

As Heim (17, p. 33) was told by the inmates he interviewed, the small group is "the place to go deeper into problems, to get at the motivations, the feelings, the 'why's' of the behavior brought up in the large group." Yet, even in the small group, there may be hesitance or resistance to discussing some of the feelings or attitudes such as those which relate to problems of sexual adjustment, like homosexuality. Therefore, according to Jones (19, p. 39) and other authorities on the correctional community, the small group must not only continue but must be supported by individual casework. The one-to-one relationship of the inmate and his counselor provides the opportunity to discuss those problems which the inmates are afraid or unwilling to bring up even in small groups. Whether, as time goes on and their security grows, they will be willing to bring even these into the large group depends upon the development of inmate trust and confidence in the community program. However, until then, small groups provide greater versatility for meeting individual needs.

No one form of the correctional community has yet been universally accepted. One would hope that this very promising, new program would not settle down in its infancy into a fixed pattern of structures and operations. It should continue to remain open for further extensive trial and experimentation in correctional institutions.

PETER F. OSTWALD

THE INTERVIEW

The personal interview is an important tool for studying and modifying behavior of inmates in a correctional community. Well-conducted interviews can enhance communication opened up through the group program, while clumsy, inept interviewing can disrupt it. Our heavy reliance on group process sometimes obscures the need for individual relationships, and interviewing partly fulfills this need. Only in the interview relationship can a staff member get a close look at the individual problems of an inmate. Indeed, a staff member must be able to understand and to master the two-person interview before he can deal effectively with the dynamics of an entire group.

Interviews are scheduled meetings between two individuals, usually at a preset place and time. Everything that happens to the participants during this time is part of the interview. Informal chance meetings between inmate and staff member, like a passing greeting or exchange of pleasantries, are not considered interviews, even though such activities may help the two persons to acknowledge and recognize each other, and this may influence the climate of subsequent interviews. On the other hand, so long as the inmate is with the staff member during the scheduled time, this is an interview, even though it can happen that there is little talking because much of the time is spent in silent communication. Interviews may be scheduled by mutual consent when both participants want to meet. In this event both know fairly well what to expect from one another, what questions are likely to come up, and what topics need to be explored. However, it is also possible that interviews are set up on the initiative of one of the participants when he has a problem, for example an inmate who needs advice or a staff member who has to have particular information. In such instances there may be less mutuality, and the person who takes the initiative has to dispel anticipatory anxiety by indicating the purpose of this scheduled meeting.

How the interview is conducted and what happens during the time spent together will reflect whether the interview is a mutual enterprise or a one-sided operation. It is important to remember that in any large institution—hospital, school, or correctional facility—the clients outnumber the staff. Partly for this reason, the scheduling of interviews is controlled by the interviewer, whose time is usually limited by other demands for his service. This gives the interviewer a superior status and carries with it the responsibility for doing whatever he can to get the meeting off to a good start, even though the request for the interview may originally have come from the interviewed person.

Interviews are especially useful at times of transition when inmates and staff personnel are likely to experience the greatest tensions. For example, when a new man first enters the community, interviews can help him adjust to the strange environment and can also help the staff get acquainted with him. Any time when negative forces threaten the continuity of the group work—for instance because of delinquent acting-out by a particularly difficult inmate—personal interviews are needed to forestall and reduce clique formations. Before the inmate is released from the community on parole, when he returns after the first visit with his family, or when he is transferred to another institution, interviews help reduce the emotional turbulence stirred up whenever old interpersonal ties have to be dissolved and new ones established.

STARTING THE INTERVIEW

Beginnings of interviews are important because of the jelling effect they create on what is to follow. Many people think that interviews start with talking, when one of the participants asks the first question or makes the first comment. But actually by the time this happens the interview is already under way. The real start of an interview is a visual encounter, a mutual appraisal of feelings and intentions that precede the opening verbal exchanges. Inmate and staff member quickly look at each other for nonverbal signs of tension, angry feelings, friendly attitudes and other subtle emotional nuances. The visual cues most revealing of a person's unspoken expectations and feelings are concentrated in the face, especially the eyes and the region around the nose and lips. Because the face is so richly endowed with expressive muscles, some people develop a "poker-faced" attitude, or obscure part of the face with a cigarette or pipe, or by holding their chin in such a way that the corners of the mouth are covered up. The hands, the shoulders, posture of the body, and movements and positions of the legs and feet may also reveal information about feelings and attitudes. In this regard it is important to keep sociocultural differences in mind. For example, an inmate raised in an Italian-American family may use and interpret hand gestures quite differently from an American Negro.

Almost invariably the initial encounter is used to review silently the expectations held before the interview. For instance, an inmate may enter the interview expecting to be punished for a delinquency not known to the staff member. The guilty man may confront a smiling, friendly staff member who is caught off guard. When there is mutual deeper suspiciousness, friendliness may be seen as a mask which hides a punitive attitude. This creates an emotional climate of fear and tension that influences whatever the participants subsequently say and hear.

We usually emphasize the importance of the *inmate's* initial visual reactions to the interviewer rather than vice versa. In a professional interview the inmate knows much less about the staff member than the other way around. The staff member has access to legal documents, prison work-ups, medical and psychological reports, and parole and violation records about the inmate, whose only knowledge of the staff member is what has been learned firsthand through previous personal contacts or secondhand through the grapevine. This inequality in terms

of background information about each other is another factor
that can increase the tension and make the inmate look at
the staff member as "top dog" in the interview.

The spoken portion of the interview includes more than an
exchange of words which carry semantic meaning. An equally
important aspect of speech is the voice used by the speaker to
project his thoughts. Words and voice, although inseparable,
carry different kinds of information. It may be necessary to
attend selectively to one or the other component of the conversation.

Voice belongs to a speaker's personality. It expresses his
feelings and is geared to the physiological processes of breath-
ing and phonation (vocal cord vibration) over which he has
relatively little conscious control. The sound of the voice also
depends on the shape and structure of the chest, head, throat,
and mouth. It is therefore possible to identify a person on the
basis of his voice, a physical property which can be objecti-
fied by sound spectrograms, or "voice prints." Words in speech
have much more to do with one's learning and education. What
a person says reflects where he has lived, who his parents were,
what languages he learned, the influence of his teachers, and
various occupational and professional roles held throughout
life.

An interviewer should listen carefully to both the voice and
word content of speech when he conducts an interview. Who
starts the talking and what exactly is said may matter less than
the quality of attention and selection used in listening. If the
staff member is the first to speak, he should listen not only to
his own words, sentences, and meanings, but give equal attention to the sound of his voice—its loudness, pitch, rhythm, and
tone quality. His voice will have a reinforcing effect on the
inmate's emotional reactions, affirming or negating some of
the initial impressions based on visual and gestural cues. The
inmate's willingness to confide in and trust the staff member,
or his eagerness to clam up and remain on guard will through-

out the interview be influenced by what he sees in the interviewer's face and hears in his voice.

Similarly, if the inmate starts the conversation, selective attentiveness to both his voice and his words will often pay off. Pauses, gasping for air, flat uninflected pitch, a harsh or raspy voice quality, the absence or abundance of rhythmic stress accents are all valuable acoustic cues for sizing up how uncomfortable a person is feeling. The better the staff member gets to know an inmate the easier it will be to find out by listening to his voice whether he is sick or well, full of energy or depressed, friendly or angry. Opening remarks of an interview are especially important for this kind of diagnostic listening because the inmate has not as yet had a chance to get adjusted to the personal attitudes of the staff member. Initial statements are apt to reflect more closely what was felt and anticipated before the interview began. Some language experts feel that just about everything which is of any real importance gets communicated during "the first five minutes" of an interview and that whatever happens thereafter has to do with clarification, organization, and utilization of this information.

THE INTERVIEW CONTRACT

One of the most important elements to be clarified is the purpose of the interview, the goals toward which inmate and staff member are consciously trying to work. In this respect interviews should not confer on either participant the right to limit his communicative behavior, as may be the case with interrogations where the staff member is obliged to ask the questions whereas the inmate is expected to answer. Interviews also differ from psychotherapy, where the patient is expected to carry the conversational ball much of the time while the doctor may remain largely silent. Interview conversations are true dialogues which allow the participants to share their correctional interests on an equal footing. This equality of interests is the initial contract—the agreement to be candid and honest about the problem at hand.

While it may look simple enough, such a contract is often hard for the inmate to understand and for the staff member to enforce.

Strict adherence to the interview contract may be difficult. For example, an angry, truculent, self-punitive inmate may only be able to go so far as to agree to sit sullenly through the allotted interview time. If he cannot agree to talk, as you expect him to, it is foolish to pretend otherwise by engaging in chit-chat. After a while, he may agree to say certain things about himself, but nothing about the other inmates. Or he may agree to talk about his mother but not his father. Sometimes it is necessary for the inmate to be repeatedly reminded of the contractual nature of the interview, so that when the contract is lived up to the interviewer can give him credit for this accomplishment and when the contract is broken can criticise him for it. Only in this way may a severely antisocial person gradually be able to develop a degree of trust and confidence in his interviewer, a quality of good feeling that hopefully will spread to his relationships with other staff members as well.

Especially when things look bleak—which happens often in the life of the seriously disturbed or recidivistic inmate—a helpful approach is to look for possible agreements and to spell out contractual possibilities. For example, there are men whose negativism and suspiciousness makes them want to argue and disagree all the time. In interviews with such inmates, you may be able to clear the air by saying things like "OK, let's agree to disagree" or "well, we can at least agree on one thing, which is that you don't want to talk to me." This is not only a way of acknowledging reality. It also shows the inmate that the interviewer is not afraid of facing what is going on in this interview and that he can withstand feelings and inner tensions without getting "mad," going "crazy" or acting-out in a delinquent way. By watching his interviewer go through this process without becoming upset, an inmate can begin to build up his own resistances against disruptive behavior. This may be one of the first steps in the inmate's identifying with the staff member, a step which has to be taken over and over again if the interview is to become a corrective experience.

THE INTERPERSONAL RELATIONSHIP

Interviews that proceed satisfactorily allow the participants gradually to establish a personal relationship. The feeling of personal relatedness grows more intense when there is a sequence of successful interviews at weekly or biweekly intervals. Interpersonal relationships kindle strong emotions which can be related to the realities of the interview itself. For instance, an inmate whose parole has just been denied may turn his pent-up anger on the staff member who interviews him, unleashing a barrage of hostile accusations that had to be held back at the official parole board meeting. Unless the staff member is prepared for this and has information about what happened to trigger the inmate's attack, he runs the risk of himself bristling with reactive distress or even reciprocating in a revengeful way.

In addition to the more obvious frustrations likely to inflame personal relationships formed in correctional communities, feelings and attitudes that actually have little to do with immediate reality may also have to be tackled. Pent-up emotions derive from memories of past life difficulties which are now recalled in the setting of confinement. For example, the inmate's frustration at being denied parole may awaken reminiscences of very painful disappointments in early childhood. These memories often are incomplete and fragmentary, and the traumatic experiences themselves may have been repressed, so that the associated feelings do not become too unbearable. Personal histories of many inmates include extremely disagreeable childhood experiences like loss of parents and disintegration of the family. Overwhelming emotional reactions of grief, despair, rage, and attack that were part of these earlier calamities can occur again in an attenuated fashion in all subsequent human relationships of any importance, especially when the inmate is reminded in word or deed of the nature of the earlier deprivations.

The correctional interview should not try to deal too directly with the emotional wear and tear of past tragedies that cannot be undone. Instead, the focus usually has to be on more recent

avoidable events which precipitate troubles that may be re-
versed. Interviews must try first of all to look candidly at the
present life of the inmate, with its daily headaches, frustrations, and dilemmas. Repetitious elaboration of past memories
or utopian fantasies may even interfere with the interview's
important goal of reality-testing. An inmate may want to dis-
play his battle scars in order to distract the interviewer from
some current problem in his behavior which he is afraid to discuss. The interviewer should certainly not ignore such evasive
tactics. The best way to handle them is to acknowledge that he
knows about the many injustices which the inmate already en-
dured. But instead of dwelling on the inmate's past misfortunes,
he should be told about the job of discussing the present-day
reality which comes first. This directness helps dissolve interpersonal ambiguity and confusion, which are qualities of dis-
torted human interactions from which many inmates have had
to suffer.

Definition of the staff member's role helps the interpersonal
relationship evolve along realistic lines. There may be times
when wishful and magical thinking causes inmates to expect
far more from interviews than can be accomplished. For example, some may want the interviews to straighten out their
marital problems, others to hear predictions of employment opportunities, all of which relate to intangibles outside the prison
over which the staff personnel may have no control. Such re-
quests or intimations of power can sometimes be flattering. It
is well to be on guard against this and to avoid promises which
cannot be kept. This holds true for matters inside the correctional community as well. The group meetings will help clarify
the functional responsibilities of the staff members but such
definitions may be temporarily forgotten in the heat of a personal interview. If some misunderstanding about the staff member's role is allowed to persist—in regard to privileges, transfers,
job assignments, or progress reports—he risks disappointing,
even infuriating, the inmate, whose tolerance for frustration
is usually low from the start. On the other hand, the staff member should not belittle himself merely for the reason that he
is unable to grant the inmate everything he wants. If pride and

integrity about work in the correctional community is not stead-
fastly maintained, the inmate whose own sense of self-esteem
is low may become pessimistic and embittered toward the interview relationship.

When the inmate is talking and the staff member listens re-
flectively, it may happen that spontaneous inner thoughts reach
the staff member's awareness, for example: "Hey, that's a really
amazing story—I'd like to hear more—go on" or "Oh no! not
that old crap again—I've heard it a million times already—shut
up." These are inner dialogues, a kind of abbreviated conversational process taking place between a person and himself.
Every child growing up goes through a phase of talking audibly
to himself, but later this self-dialogue is gradually internalized
and goes on mostly in silence. Occasionally, while one privately
rehearses a talk before giving it in public, inner dialogues again
are spoken out, for instance in comments like "Gee, that
sounded good" or "Hell, it didn't make sense—try it again."

Inner dialogues can help the interview by guiding such crucial decisions as when to continue listening and when to inter-
rupt. There are no cookbook rules for the conduct of interviews;
each follows a unique pattern, unpredictable to a certain extent.
Outsiders watching the interview through an observation screen
notice only the external conversations between inmate and staff
member. The inner dialogues, of equal relevance for understanding the dynamics of the interaction, are directly perceived
only by the participants themselves. Noticeably, as the inmate
becomes an important person, the things he tells the staff member begin to echo inside his listening mind. It is as if the inmate took a place inside the interviewer, who in turn were
introjected into the inmate's mind. These "inside-outsiders" become the partners in inner dialogues, helping the conversation
by giving spontaneous cues, ideas, and insights. The inner dialogue can try out different comments, questions, admonitions,
or compliments in advance, before these are uttered openly,
perhaps inappropriately, thus embarrassing or insulting the

inmate and causing him to withdraw. For example, the inner
dialogue may ask "Do you know who stole that screwdriver
from the machine shop?" Another internal voice may then say,
"OK—ask!—he can take it"—which permits the question to be
articulated openly. At another time, this kind of question might
be squelched by an internal warning of "better not ask it this
way—he'll just deny his behavior—the question really sounds
like an accusation." In the imaginative inner dialogue the interviewer can take the inmate's point of view and rehearse
questions or comments without blurting them out. Each interview is an emotional experience as well as an intellectual one,
and the interviewer may be stumped trying to "figure out" only
in logical terms what is happening. There is no coach to tell
him what to do next, nor will another inmate, as in group therapy, join the conversation. Reliance on the inner dialogue can
sometimes help get an interviewer over a deadlock, and by
attending to any concomitant visual fantasies he may be able
to recall things of importance that happened during a previous
interview with the inmate. Such memories can help provide
continuity with the current interview. Also this kind of listening with the inner ear may help bring up novel, meaningful,
and spontaneous formulations toward the end of an interview,
when separation becomes a problem.

The inmate too has inner dialogues, but the interviewer will
not be able to hear these unless he can get this preconscious
material to be translated into outer conversational speech. It
is not easy to do this in a correctional setting where many
inmates may be men of action rather than of words. Their
inner dialogues may be full of curses, oaths, and other expressions of hostility which can only be brought out in the presence of the other inmates or when the man is alone. Secrets,
fears, magical or "crazy" ideas which the inmate is afraid to
reveal may be deliberately held back. Sometimes there are
prayerful, childlike, sexual or loving themes which embarrass
the inmate too much to allow for externalization in speech. If
this happens he may start to talk compulsively, producing a
repetitious and monotonous outer speech to hide painful or
embarrassing inner dialogues from himself and the interviewer.

The group meeting is an important safety valve for unexpres-
sible preoccupations because here it may be possible for one
inmate to say what is on another man's mind, shielding the
other and himself from the pain of self-revelation.

The end of an interview can be difficult because of its symbolic
resemblance to past painful separations. Since separation in-
volves two people the staff member must be sensitive to his
own role in all types of separations. This issue comes up in
group meetings too—whenever someone is transferred, goes on
vacation, or leaves the institution—but closing of individual
interviews stimulates separation anxiety much more intensely
and provides a good training ground for understanding this
problem.

Usually closing takes place when the allotted interview time
is used up. This matter of time is of utmost importance, especially to the inmate. His "time" in the correctional institution
has been set by others, and he may resent being reminded that
he is not in control of time and therefore not of himself. The
closing of each interview and the end of the interview relationship can be an unconscious reminder of this kind of personal insignificance.

Sometimes the only way to deal with the problem is by
being very matter-of-fact and simply saying "Well, our time is
up, we'll meet again next week." This not only reminds the
inmate of the reality of impersonal time but also gives him
something to look forward to. The other dimension, the personal sense of readiness to quit, is more difficult to assess. When
the question comes up, it is well for the staff member to check
both the inmate's and his own introspective time sense, the
inner clocks of mood and feeling. Every living creature has
these internal clocking devices which control and coordinate
his behavior. There is evidence to suggest that the inmates of
prisons and the patients of mental hospitals cannot successfully
correlate their internal time systems to those of so-called
healthy, or normal, people. However this may be, it always

is beneficial if the staff member asks the inmate and himself whether it *feels* right to quit. This strategy will help keep the interview focussed on its mutuality. Just as each interview must close with some reference to the future, as "see you next week," the end of the interview relationship, terminated by departure from the institution, should also bridge the uncertainty of the future. This is done by the use during the last hours together in discussion of plans for parole, return to work, re-establishment of family life, and other goals of life outside the institution.

When an interview relationship has been particularly useful and friendly, the inmate may on occasion wish to prolong it by writing letters, calling up, or sending messages back to the staff member. There is no need to act stand-offish if this happens, although it is always important to remind the released inmate that any new problems have to be discussed with his parole officer. Once the formal interview relationship has come to an end, a certain amount of informal friendly contact is certainly permissible. Usually however, the reality of pressures of new responsibilities make this impractical for the staff member, and the released man himself prefers to start a new life outside, which does not remind him too often of experiences "behind the walls."

John P. Conrad

THE EVALUATION OF THE
CORRECTIONAL COMMUNITY

Traditional institutional management responsive to public and legislative concerns has stoutly resisted change. As long as troubles were not evident to outsiders, the institution was thought to be doing its job. If too many inmates escaped or serious violence or riots occurred, prisons were criticized. The evaluation of correctional institutions as good or bad used to be that simple.

Today, the evaluation of correctional institutions is less shallow. A steady stream of books, plays, television and radio programs, and public discussions testifies to widespread interest. Any new program is subject to evaluation, both by members of the correctional system and by social scientists.

In evaluating the correctional community, we must find ways of determining whether it is achieving what it sets out to produce. Its primary goal is to restore the delinquent or criminal to the community without endangering the public. Our problem is to measure how effective the program is in influencing offenders. In California, the Department of Corrections has been experimenting with the correctional community for several years. The program has been developed in somewhat different ways in different places, which adds to the difficulties in trying to evaluate its usefulness.

Many optimistic evaluative comments about the therapeutic community have come from the mental hospital where the program has a much longer history. Implicit in the publications of Jones, Wilmer, Rapoport, Cummings, Stanton, Schwartz, and others is their faith in the concepts and methods of the therapeutic community in the mental hospital. A volume published by the Mental Health Department of Massachusetts (9) illustrates the likelihood of favorable findings when researches have been completed. The authors, authorities in psychiatry, psychology, and sociology, believe that future studies will confirm the values of the therapeutic community in mental hospitals.

At this early stage of correctional-community treatment, the faith of the innovator is essential. But faith must be accompanied by the study of consequences. Faith runs dry when results are unknown. The researcher who evaluates is essential to the faith of the innovator.

THE MEANING OF EVALUATION

Evaluation means to find out the usefulness of somebody or something. Usefulness for what? We must know what goal is to be achieved, and how. In short, there must be a theory.

Suppose that we are orange growers interested in increasing the size of oranges. We know that nitrogen applied in certain amounts to the soil will increase the size of some varieties of plants. We theorize that if we apply a certain amount of nitrogenous fertilizer to our trees at a certain time of the year, oranges will grow larger. Now we could use the fertilizer according to our theory, and if the oranges were bigger than last year's, we would wonder whether the difference might just as well be attributed to a milder winter, less smog, more rain, or other influences. If we want to test our theory critically, we would probably use the fertilizer in one part of the grove and not in another, but both would be cultivated in the same way. If we get larger oranges next year, it would evidence that the fertilizer was probably responsible. We could then decide whether the money spent on the fertilizer was offset by the price for the premium-size oranges.

People are more complex than orange trees and a correctional facility is more complex than an orange grove but the principle is the same. The problem of evaluating a prison program is to find what difference the use of the program makes to inmates.

The problem is not as simple as taking half the inmates in a correctional facility and giving them a special correctional community program, then taking the other half and giving them the conventional program, and then waiting for a few years to see how many from each group fail. You expect a difference in favor of the correctional-community group, but the chances are that you will not find it. And if you do find a difference, what does it mean? Do you draw the conclusion that all inmates in all correctional institutions should be subjected to correctional-community programs? What assurance do you have that there were no other significant differences between the two groups? What accounts for those inmates in the community group who failed? What accounts for the inmates in the "control group" who succeeded?

STEPS IN THE EVALUATIVE PROCESS

Several steps should be taken before we can conclude that the correctional-community program is beneficial. First, there must be a theory. The theory says that peer group influences on peer behavior in a well-run community may change behavior favorably. To maximize these influences we need a medium of communication that will reach all the inmates—a daily meeting of the inmates, the large group described in earlier chapters. In the large group the staff and inmates emerge as social beings living together with the common objective of resocializing the inmates. In the group meeting the day by day social experiences of the members will be the subject of frank discussions from which they are expected to learn enough about the consequences of their behavior that they will *want* to change to get along successfully in a normal community.

Our second step is to design a model. When will this daily meeting occur, and for how long? We suggest 8:30 A.M. because people are rested then and ready for the reminder that everything that happens to them during the day must be considered in the light of its significance for treatment. And we suggest an hour and a half because we have noticed that it usually takes fifteen or twenty minutes for a group to settle down and a period of less than an hour is not enough for the desired freedom of interaction.

It soon becomes evident that there are many facets which must be considered in evaluating a program. When the model is planned in detail, we have a correctional community which can be evaluated.

THE DEVELOPMENT OF THE TESTING PROGRAM

To develop a model for testing, the number of inmates and staff, the qualifications of the staff, the frequency of the meetings, the lengths of the programs must be determined. The rules or limits must be established and the methods of enforcement prescribed. Program content must be decided. Finally, agreement must be reached on the standards for evaluating successful completion of the program.

During the first months the model can only be observed, not fairly tested. If we are to achieve a valid research evaluation, the researchers should be on hand to see what are the problems in getting the necessary information. If the model needs changes in order to get this information, this is the time when changes should be made.

It is also the time to make operational changes. Suppose sixty inmates meet in the dayroom every morning at 8:30. We can get them together satisfactorily but because of the noise in the corridor and the bad acoustics in the room some members of the group cannot hear what is being said. This calls for some practical adjustment.

During the period of the pilot run changes can be made. When the program is jelled in a defined plan, changes would interfere with the evaluation.

After the trial run, and after revisions have been made, we decide that as of a certain day the program and the evaluation procedures will begin. In planning the evaluation, we select a control group as much like the experimental group as possible, which will not go through the experience designed for the experimental model. Both groups are observed by the research staff and reports are written. By comparing them eventually, we try to find out what makes for differences.

The research evaluation begins with recorded observations. A record is kept of the information needed to state what happened, how, why, where, and to whom. This information should at least establish that the model is being carried out; if there are deviations, they are known and recorded. Suppose there was an outbreak of influenza, and for two weeks fifteen inmates were hospitalized. This must be recorded instead of being half-remembered two years later when the attempt is made to understand why, for example, so few members of the group were favorably recommended to the Parole Board in the following month.

Much information can be punched into cards and recorded in a data-processing system. In this way at the end of the study totals can be readily obtained, comparisons can be made, and findings can be submitted supported by numerical data which help to indicate whether the program made a difference. If we have planned well, we can say how much difference it made, in what classes of inmates, and why it made a difference.

However, to evaluate the communication between staff and inmates, the researcher must observe and record. For example, the model provides that everyone in the unit must attend the 8:30 A.M. community meeting. The machines can compile the number of those who attended and those who were absent. Even the reasons for the absences can be punched into the cards. But what happened in this meeting? What topics were discussed, for how long, by how many, and by whom? Did the discussion tie in with yesterday's session, or was a stirring topic from a stormy session a week ago revived? The questions are limited only by the imagination of the researchers and their colleagues on the staffs of the experimental and control units. Ingenious methods have been devised to study the effects of seating arrangements or interactions or to keep track of the number of interactions each member of the group had with each of the other members. If we decide that it is important enough, this kind of information can also be coded and recorded on cards for data-processing.

The importance of the detailed contents of the research design becomes more evident where the evaluative study is in operation. The model cannot be expected to operate mechanically like an engine, because human beings cannot adequately be predicted and diagrammed. Sometimes the model will be functioning about the way it was intended to do; however, we must also record what happens at less satisfying times. We need to record when some aggressive inmate intimidated enough group members to reduce intragroup communication, the group's uneasiness because the superintendent has, without prior notice, routed a stream of foreign visitors through the unit, the hostility aroused in the group by a new staff member.

Some of these distortions are brief enough to make no significant difference. Others may produce enduring changes in the meeting. For a fair evaluation we need to know everything that interferes with its proper functioning. We have only to think of the differences in the functioning of the experimental group under a bright, well-trained, and enthusiastic staff as compared with an apathetic, frequently absent, untrained group of time servers.

CRITERIA OF SUCCESS

We are so accustomed to thinking of rates of recidivism as the yardstick of success in corrections that we forget that there are other ways of determining the success of a tested program. Recidivism alone does not tell enough. Nor does it tell anything at all until months and years have passed. We must open our eyes to other yardsticks.

If the theory is effectively applied in our model, we believe that attitudes should change. If we administer questionnaires and opinion surveys at well-spaced intervals, perhaps we will get some clues about these changes. If the same questionnaires are administered to members of the control group, some comparisons may be possible concerning the influences of the model, the program under study.

An important area of study and observation is the interaction among staff and inmates, inmates and inmates, and staff and staff. These studies should be made in all places in which interactions occur, in and out of formal group settings. If, as we expect, there are differences in content and frequency in the data collected in the experimental group from these same data accumulated in the control group, what are these differences? Are they consistent with the theory on which the model is based?

The large-group meeting is a laboratory in which many evaluations can be made. Is it functioning as a medium of communication for the unit as a whole, or is it restricted to interactions among a few dominant or articulate members? Do the contents of the discussions relate to issues of concern in the community, or are the sessions concerned with unimportant matters? Is the quality of the discussion consistent with the objective—the resocialization of the inmates in the group?

Finally, we must watch for the most significant, but often the most elusive measurement: evidence of changes in individual inmates. This evidence is usually obtained from members of the staff. Sometimes case records will reveal it. Yet this evidence is generally inadequate, for case records are made with various objects in mind. Work supervisors' reports of a consistent change in an inmate's attitudes may be useful. Teachers may not see a marked improvement in inmates' grades. Or the record may reveal that an inmate said in a large group session: "Last year, I would have clobbered the guy for doing that to me; now I'm bringing it up in the group for you guys to help me settle." We can look up his record and discover that, sure enough, last year he had "clobbered" another inmate for a similar action against him.

The kinds of observations mentioned make possible the completion of the essential business of linking process to outcome. If the process is sound, the outcome should be consistent with the theory. Everyone needs to know whether the correctional community is effective. Those who work in such communities must know how they work. They must know when they are working well, when they need minor repairs, and when they need a major overhaul.

So far, we have described briefly the course of evaluation for a correctional-community model. But there are many possible models. The test of one will not tell enough about the validity of the programs developed according to other models. At this stage of development of the theory, each should be studied individually. There are some important issues to be represented by the differences in the models. Some, like the following issues, could be settled: How large should a correctional-community group be? Of what kind of sample should it be composed? What is the function of individual counseling in a setting where the large group is the primary communications medium? Is the small group compatible with the community group? If so, what does it contribute? Without an evaluative study, we cannot answer these questions. And until they are answered we cannot say anything definite about the basic value of the therapeutic community.

The status of our current scientific evaluation of the correctional community is discouraging. Until the present time, there have been no satisfactory studies offering the essential data regarding the effects upon the inmates exposed to the correctional community.

The reason for the difficulty in obtaining an appraisal of the values of the correctional community is the large number of variables. Studies of a program like the correctional community, which deal with the effects of a multifactored environmental situation upon human beings, cannot be carried out like studies in the physical sciences. Therefore, in offering any kind of evaluation, we are forced for the time being to consider subjective judgments about the correctional community.

Many persons who have lived in institutions before and after the correctional-community program was introduced, are deeply convinced by their experiences that this program brings about desirable changes in the human relationships and in the emotional climate of these places. Some of these observers feel that the better interpersonal relationships in the community living groups, the greater maturity evidenced among the inmates, come about as a result of the program.

The literature contains favorable comments by persons who have worked in the correctional-community program. Reimer and Smith (25) report improved behavior among inmates following eighteen months' experience with a correctional community. Briggs in an unpublished manuscript about the Pine Hall Project has reported (5) that "during the final two years of the project, there were no escapes and no serious incidents in the housing unit, where prior to this time the unit averaged over two escapes per year and had several serious incidents that required assistance." Briggs and other workers also feel, in general, on the basis of follow-up contacts with parolees, that the parole statistics may be at least as favorable and perhaps better for the inmates exposed to the program as for comparable groups who have not had this experience.

Another significant variable in studying the effect of the correctional community concerns changes in staff attitudes brought about as a result of their participation in the program. Staff members confess to being anxious and even frustrated when first exposed to the program. This feeling has been called by Maxwell Jones, the "trauma of entry." If they survive these disturbances, and not all do, then changes occur. They become intrigued by the program, read about it, talk with colleagues, and participate eagerly in the post-sessions and other training experiences. As a result, their orientation toward inmates changes; for example, they look upon them with greater respect and consider more thoughtfully what they have to say. Their role concepts undergo serious alterations as their notions of the meaning and use of authority are revised. As the inmates demonstrate their competence in greater self-direction and more sincere interpersonal relations, their expectations of inmate behavior are no longer overclouded with suspicion and fear.

Only the actual experience of working in a correctional community can confirm or repudiate these subjective reports of the staff members. Some staff members do not change, and not all changes will be beneficial to all staff members and all inmates. Yet one cannot help being impressed by the comments of Rex Deal, an administrator of a 600-inmate unit, who began his career in corrections in a walled prison. He has actively participated in the community program for a number of years. In a paper mimeographed for staff use at the California Institution for Men, he summarized his observations as follows: "There is as yet little objective 'proof'; however, daily contacts give encouraging evidence of change; e.g., the inmate who joined the unit a few months earlier with strong resentment toward authority may be found defending the actions of a correctional officer or a Forestry foreman. A member may voluntarily divulge behavior of which only he is aware—but feels may be detrimental to his future. The examples are endless and demonstrated almost daily. Staff and inmates must rely on subjective measures to reinforce their feeling of job accomplishment. If their loyalty, interest, concern and enthusiasm are any criterion of program worth, one would not hesitate to assume that statistical measures will further demonstrate the efficacy of the 'correctional community.' "

1. Aichhorn, A. *Wayward Youth*, New York: Viking, 1935, 236 pp.
2. Bateson, G. "Analysis of Group Therapy in Admission Ward," U.S. Naval Hospital, Oakland, California. Quoted in 36, p. 346.
3. Briggs, D. L. "A Therapeutic Community in an Overseas Naval Hospital," *Military Medicine*, 122:4, April 1955.
4. Briggs, D. L. and J. M. Dowling "Administrative Requirements For a Therapeutic Community." California Institution for Men, Chino, California: 1963. Mimeographed, 13 pp.
5. Briggs, D. L. "Beyond the Devil's Hole: Perspectives on a Transitional Community Treatment Approach for Youthful Offenders." San Francisco State College, San Francisco, California. Unpublished manuscript, 1964.
6. Campbell, W. "An Incident in a Correctional Community," The California Institution for Men, Chino, California: 1964, 4 pp.
7. Chamlee, F. "Introduction of the Therapeutic Community Units," The California Institution for Men, Chino, California: 1964. Mimeographed, 22 pp.
8. Cressey, D. R. and J. Irvin. "Thieves, Convicts and the Inmate Culture," *Social Problems*, 10:2, 1962.
9. Dyken, J. W., R. W. Hyde, L. H. Orzack, and R. H. York. *Strategies of Mental Hospital Change.* State Department of Mental Health, Boston, Mass.: 1964, 187 pp.
10. Fenton, N. *An Introduction to Group Counseling in State Correctional Service.* The Department of Corrections, Sacramento, California: 1957, 204 pp. Revised edition, 1965.
11. Fenton, N., E. A. Taron, et al., eds. *Training Staff For Program Development in Youth Correctional Institutions.* Sacramento, California: Institute for the Study of Crime and Delinquency, 1965, 186 pp.
12. Goffman, Erving. *Asylums, Essays on the Social Situation of Mental Patients and Other Inmates.* New York, Doubleday: 1961, 386 pp.
13. Grant, J. D. "It's Time to Start Counting," *Crime and Delinquency*, 1962:8, pp. 259–264.
14. Greenblatt, M., York, R. H. and E. L. Brown. *From Custodial to Therapeutic Patient Care in Mental Hospitals.* New York: Russell Sage Foundation, 1955, 497 pp.

15. Hadley, J. M. *Clinical and Counseling Psychology*. New York: Knopf, 1958, 682 pp.
16. Henderson, R. D. "Interviewing: An Art and Technique," *Personnel Administration*. 2:27, 1948.
17. Heim, R. B. *Perceptions and Reactions of Prison Inmates to Two Therapeutic Communities*. Sacramento, California: The Institute For The Study of Crime and Delinquency, 1964, 96 pp.
18. Jones, M. *The Therapeutic Community*. New York: Basic Books, 1953, 186 pp.
19. Jones, M. *Social Psychiatry*. Springfield, Illinois: C. C. Thomas, 1962, 129 pp.
20. Main, T. F. *Hospital as a Therapeutic Institution*. Bulletin, Menninger Clinic, Topeka, Kansas: 1946, 10:66–70.
21. Marcuse, F. L., ed. *Areas of Psychology*. New York: Harper, 1954, 532 pp.
22. Menninger, K. A. *Manual for Psychiatric Case Study*. New York: Grune and Stratton, 1952, 355 pp.
23. Polsky, H. W. *Cottage Six*. New York: Russell Sage Foundation, 1962, 193 pp.
24. Rapoport, R. M. *The Community as Doctor*. Springfield, Illinois: C. C. Thomas, 1960, 325 pp.
25. Reimer, E. G. and G. B. Smith. "A Treatment Experience in Prison Community Living," *American Journal of Corrections*, 26:1, 1964.
26. Schmidt, D. G. *Development of Group Psychotherapy at San Quentin*. California State Prison, San Quentin, California. Group Counseling Newsletter, August 1958.
27. Schrag, C. "Some Foundations for a Theory of Corrections," in *The Prison: Studies in Institutional Organization and Change*. Donald R. Cressey, ed.: Holt, Rinehart and Winston, 1961, 392 pp.
28. Sivadon, Paul. *Techniques of Sociotherapy*. Walter Reed Symposium on Preventative and Social Psychiatry: 1958.
29. Smith, W. H. "Narcotic Treatment Control Unit." Chino, California: 1963. Mimeographed, 6 pp.
30. Spergel, I. "A Multidimensional Model for Social Work Practice: The Youth Worker Example," *Social Service Review*, 36, 1962, pp. 62–71.
31. Stanton, A. H. and M. S. Schwartz. *The Mental Hospital*. New York: Basic Books, 1954, 492 pp.
32. Stevenson, I. "The Psychiatric Interview" in *American Handbook of Psychiatry*, Arieti S., ed., New York: Basic Books, 1959, I, 197.

33. Sullivan, C. E., Grant, J. D. and M. Q. Grant. *Delinquency Integration*. Second Technical Report, Rehabilitation Research, Camp Elliott, San Diego, California, 1954.

34. Sullivan, H. S. *The Psychiatric Interview*. New York: W. W. Norton, 1954, 246 pp.

35. Sykes, Gresham M. *The Society of Captives*. Princeton University Press, 1958. Princeton, New Jersey, 144 pp.

36. Vinter, R. D. and M. Janowitz. *The Comparative Study of Juvenile Correctional Institutions*. A Research Report. Ann Arbor, Michigan: School of Social Work, University of Michigan, 1961.

37. Wilmer, H. A. *Social Psychiatry in Action*, Springfield, Illinois: C. C. Thomas, 1958, 373 pp.

www.ingramcontent.com/pod-product-compliance
Lightning Source LLC
Chambersburg PA
CBHW052012270326
41929CB00015B/2893